ACLS History E-Book Project
Reprint Series

The ACLS History E-Book Project (www.historyebook.org) collaborates with constituent societies of the American Council of Learned Societies, publishers, librarians and historians to create an electronic collection of works of high quality in the field of history. This volume is produced from digital images created for the Project by the Scholarly Publishing Office and the Digital Library Production Service at the University of Michigan, Ann Arbor. The digital reformatting process results in an electronic version of the text that can be both accessed online and used to create new print copies. This book and hundreds of others are available online in the History E-Book Project through subscription.

Many of the works in the History E-Book Project are available in print and can be ordered either directly from their publishers or as part of this series. For information refer to the online Title Record page for each book. Inquiries regarding this series can be directed to info@hebook.org.

ACLS
HISTORY E-BOOK

http://www.historyebook.org

BUSINESS HISTORY SERIES
GRADUATE SCHOOL OF BUSINESS ADMINISTRATION
NEW YORK UNIVERSITY
Thomas C. Cochran, Editor

THE MEDICI BANK

Its Organization, Management, Operations, and Decline

COSIMO DE' MEDICI, PATER PATRIAE
HEAD OF THE MEDICI BANK, 1428–1464

Marble Relief by Andrea del Verrocchio
Kaiser Friedrich Museum, Berlin

THE Medici Bank

ITS ORGANIZATION, MANAGEMENT, OPERATIONS, AND DECLINE

BY RAYMOND DE ROOVER

ASSOCIATE PROFESSOR OF ECONOMICS

WELLS COLLEGE

1948

NEW YORK

New York University Press, Washington Square

LONDON

Geoffrey Cumberlege · Oxford University Press

PRINTED IN THE UNITED STATES OF AMERICA

To N. S. B. GRAS

whose teaching inspired this study on one of the most famous business firms in history

EDITOR'S FOREWORD

DEAN G. Rowland Collins of the Graduate School of Business Administration, the godfather of this series, shares my enthusiasm in publishing Raymond de Roover's *The Medici Bank*. It is not only an important addition to the historical analysis of banking during the formative period of modern institutions, but it also helps to illustrate the intended scope of the New York University studies in business history. In course of time, we hope to publish volumes on special aspects of business and studies of the inter-reaction of individual businesses with their industry as well as the biographies of business leaders and company histories.

As Professor de Roover points out in his preface, the present book is a feat of historical archaeology. Other scholars have written of the Medici Bank, but as none brought to the task the unusual training and abilities of Professor de Roover, none was able to transmute the fragmentary records into a satisfactory picture of a going concern.

Had one the power over many years to train a scholar especially for such a task, it would be hard to improve on the education of the author. After graduating from the Institut Supérieur de Commerce in Antwerp in 1924 and completing his military training, Professor de Roover began work in a bank. Soon after, he joined the staff of the Agence Maritime Internationale, the largest steamship operating concern in Belgium and one of the largest in the world. There, ultimately in the position of *chef de service*—officer in charge of all ship accounts—he remained until 1936. During his career as a Belgian *expert comptable,* he became interested in economic history and in the history of accounting. Working in his spare time in the archives of Antwerp and Bruges, he wrote *Jan Ympyn: Essai historique et technique sur le premier traité flamand de comptabilité* (Antwerp: Veritas, 1928) and in addition published as many articles as would be expected over a similar period from one enjoying the relative leisure of an academic post. Through these articles Professor de Roover met his wife, Florence Edler, an American scholar studying European economic history on a Belgian-American Educational Foundation fellowship.

As a result of his marriage Professor de Roover decided to leave the business world and acquire the education customary for a scholar. At Harvard he studied with N. S. B. Gras and Abbott Payson Usher, won the James Bowdoin literary prize, and in June of 1938 received the degree of Master in Business Administration. In that summer Professor and Mrs. de Roover photographed the records that form the basis for this Medici Bank study. John U. Nef, Frank H. Knight, Jacob Viner, and Chester W. Wright all helped in completing Professor de Roover's formal education at the University of Chicago. His doctoral dissertation on money, banking, and credit in medieval Bruges, in greatly revised form, is in process of publication by the Mediaeval Academy of America. At present he is Associate Professor of Economics at Wells College.

In the course of this brief summary of such an unusual combination of practical European commercial training and formal education by some of America's outstanding professors, there has been no space to list the numerous articles written by both of the de Roovers. As editors of *The Journal of Economic History,* Frederic C. Lane and I had the pleasure of publishing Parts I and II of this book in a series of three articles. Professor Lane is largely responsible for initiating the idea of enlarging the work and making it available in book form. The idea, however, only became a reality through the help of Dean Collins who secured the necessary financial aid from New York University.

THOMAS C. COCHRAN

CONTENTS

Part I

Part II

Appendixes

ILLUSTRATIONS

CHARTS AND TABLES

INTRODUCTION

THIS is not the first book dealing with the Medici Bank. The pioneer work is the study of Heinrich Sieveking which was published in 1905. Sieveking's study was an outstanding achievement for its time and is still useful as a reference, despite the progress that has been made in the writing of economic and business history. The book of Otto Meltzing, which followed soon after that of Sieveking, is disappointing. It contains no new material and many mistakes which, unfortunately, have been recopied and repeated by subsequent authors. The latest work of importance is a biography of Cosimo de' Medici by Curt S. Gutkind. Although it deals with all aspects of Cosimo's eventful career, Gutkind has made a laudible effort to gain insight into the business policy of the great man who brought the Medici Bank to the summit of its size, prosperity, and power. Gutkind failed, however, to make a significant contribution, partly because he lacked proper training in business and economics and partly because he carelessly gave new currency to his predecessors' mistakes and even added a few items to the circulation of false information.

The present book endeavors to correct the defects and the shortcomings of earlier works, to give an accurate account of the organization and the management of the Medici Bank, to examine the nature of its business, and to investigate the causes of its decay under the disastrous administration of Lorenzo the Magnificent. Briefly, this study is an attempt to show how the wheels turned around in the business world of the Renaissance. The method used is the same as that which would be used in the analysis of the structure, the policies, and the history of a modern business concern—be it Macy's department store, the Pabst Brewing Company, the Burlington Railroad, or the Standard Oil.

This study is based mainly on the business records of the Medici Bank: partnership agreements, correspondence, and account books. The extant material is unfortunately fragmentary; for example, no balance sheets have survived. Only a few pages of some of the account books have escaped destruction by a frenzied mob. However, the historian, like the archaeologist, is sometimes able to reconstruct an edifice by piecing together small fragments. Some of the correspondence between the main office and the branches has been published by Armand Grunzweig in his *Correspondance de la filiale de Bruges des*

Medici. The first volume appeared in 1931, but the scholarly world is still awaiting the publication of the second. After writing to M. Grunzweig it became clear to me that this publication had been postponed *sine die.* I decided, therefore, to go ahead with my own work, although the second volume might have added new information.

Of the account books, I have used chiefly the extant fragment of the ledger of the Bruges branch for the year 1441 which I photographed in the summer of 1938 during a brief stay in Florence. The project upon which I was then working required me to spend most of my time in the Datini Archives in Prato, so that I was unable to take pictures of the other account books. Sieveking describes a ledger of the main office for 1460 but he lists only the names of some of the principal correspondents and the titles of some of the impersonal accounts. Such information is of little value. It is only by analyzing specific entries or, preferably, related entries that account books yield useful information. An analysis of some of the entries in the Bruges ledger is given in the appendixes.

This book is dedicated to Professor N. S. B. Gras of Harvard University. Before I became his student, I had done some work on the history of accounting and I was familiar with medieval methods of bookkeeping. It was Professor Gras who broadened my horizon and who taught me how to apply this knowledge and how to use accounting as a tool rather than as an end in itself.

Without the generous aid of the Belgian Fonds National de la Recherche Scientifique, which gave me a grant to do research in Italy, this study would have been impossible. I am especially indebted to Professor François L. Ganshof of the University of Ghent and to the late and much regretted scholar, Henri Laurent, who very kindly sponsored my application for a grant-in-aid. I must also mention the Director of the Archivio di Stato in Florence who made the necessary arrangements for me to photograph one Medici account book and other material under the supervision of a member of his staff.

With the exception of the appendixes and a few pages of revised text, this book is a reprint of a series of three articles which were published in *The Journal of Economic History.* I am grateful to one of the editors of this journal, Professor Frederic C. Lane of the Johns Hopkins University, who not only accepted the manuscript for publication but made many valuable suggestions for its improvement. I am especially thankful that he made me rewrite an obscure crucial passage until it was clear. I wish to thank Professor Armando Sapori of the University of Florence, who kindly made a special trip to the Archives to decipher a few words in an account which I had vainly tried to read from the microfilm in my possession. I appreciate the thoughtfulness of Professor Emeritus Ferdinand Schevill and my friend, Robert S. Lopez of Yale University, who called my attention to errors in the version which was published in *The Journal of Economic History*.

My deepest obligation is to my wife, Florence Edler de Roover, who is a scholar in her own right. I have greatly benefited from her knowledge of Italian history and her acquaintance with sources and bibliography. It was she who persuaded me to photograph the secret account book of Francesco Sassetti which had not impressed me as being of any interest but which turned out to be a document of the greatest value. Mrs. de Roover has constantly assisted me with her advice and criticism in the preparation of this study. I am indebted to her in so many ways that she should have signed this book with me. She has refused to do so but has allowed me to state that she is the sole author of Appendix IX which deals with Francesco Sassetti's portrait in the Bache Collection of the Metropolitan Museum.

I also wish to acknowledge the aid which I have received from New York University Press, especially from Miss Jean B. Barr and Miss Dorothy Beck, who have prepared the manuscript for the printer, secured better photographs for the illustrations than those I possessed, and helped make the Index.

Aurora-on-Cayuga RAYMOND DE ROOVER
January 10, 1948

Part 1

ORGANIZATION AND MANAGEMENT

§1. *The Florentine Banking System*

THE organization of a commercial firm or a corporation is usually determined by the nature of its business. We must, therefore, know the meaning of the word "bank" which appears in the title of this study. Today this word has a variety of meanings. There are all sorts of banks: central banks, commercial banks, member banks, and so forth. In the fifteenth century, there were not so many kinds of credit institutions. But still the word "bank" had more than one meaning. What kind of bank was the Medici bank?

In Florence, in the fifteenth century, there were three or four different credit institutions called banks in Italian: *banchi di pegno, banchi a minuto, banchi in mercato,* and *banchi grossi.* The first were pawnshops, operating under a public license which permitted the pawnbrokers to make loans secured by pledges of personal property at a legal rate of four pence per pound a month or 20 per cent a year. This was not a high rate of interest when we consider that today in several states of the Union the legal rate for small loans is 36 per cent per annum. The Medici bank was certainly not a pawnshop and did not specialize in consumers' credit to the poorer classes of Florence. There is presumably no direct connection, as has been supposed, between the red roundels or torteaux of the Medici coat of arms and the three balls which became the characteristic sign of pawnshops.[1]

Besides the pawnshops or *banchi di pegno,* there existed in Florence

[1] The origin of the Medici coat of arms is as obscure as that of the Medici family. Roundels are a common charge, not only in Italian but also in French and English heraldry. According to one theory, the armorial bearings of the Medici are canting arms or *armes parlantes,* and the torteaux or red balls supposedly represent pills, because *medici* in Italian means "physicians." The historian G. F. Young regards this whole story as a fable.—*The Medici,* chap. iii, n. 2. He is probably right. A more plausible explanation is that the Medici adopted the roundels because they were the symbol of the banker's trade and of the guild to which they belonged. The coat of arms of the Florentine money-changers' guild, Arte del Cambio, was a red shield sown with bezants or gold roundels. The Medici used red roundels instead of gold ones. The pawnbrokers eventually adopted the gold roundels or balls as the sign of their trade, since those symbols were associated in the public mind with money lending and credit.—Raymond de Roover, "The Three Golden Balls of the Pawnbrokers," *Bulletin of the Business Historical Society,* XX (1946), 117–24. See esp. illustrations on p. 123.

banchi a minuto or "retail banks." There is as yet little exact information available concerning the activities of these *banchi a minuto*. Francesco di Giuliano de' Medici, a distant cousin of the historic Medici, was connected with two different banks of this type from 1476 to 1491. From the extant account books of these banks it appears that the business of a *banco a minuto* consisted chiefly in the sale of jewelry on credit, according to an installment plan. Loans secured by jewels were also made. Dealings in bullion and money changing were apparently also part of the bank's activities. Only time deposits, on which interest was paid at 9 or 10 per cent, were accepted by the banks in which Francesco di Giuliano was a partner; their ledgers do not contain any accounts relating to deposits "payable on demand." Neither do the journals contain any book transfers, such as are found by the thousands in the books of the Genoese banks and of the Bruges money-changers. Consequently, a *banco a minuto* was not a deposit bank. There may be some question whether such a business should be considered as a bank at all. Francesco de' Medici, however, refers to himself and his partners sometimes as *banchieri* and sometimes as *tavolieri*.[2]

A third group of banks, called *banchi in mercato* by some of the Florentine chroniclers, is probably the same as the *banchi aperti* mentioned in the statutes of the Arte del Cambio, the money-changers' guild. Their business was done "in the open" or in the public market places of Florence, the Mercato Vecchio and the Mercato Nuovo. The owners of these banks were designated as *cambiatori* (money-changers) or as *tavolieri* because they did business sitting behind a table *(tavola)* covered with a cloth *(tappeto)*, a journal open in front of them and a money pouch *(tasca)* within reach. By statute the money-changers were required to make transfers in their books in the presence of their customers. As checks were as yet unknown, transfer orders were given by word of mouth and were written immediately in the banker's books. The guild regulations therefore suggest that the *banchi in mercato* were the transfer and deposit banks of Florence.[3]

The business of the Florentine *banchi in mercato* was similar to that

[2] I owe this information to my wife Florence Edler de Roover, who is writing a biography, "Francesco di Giuliano de' Medici (1450–1528), Business Man of Florence." Her book is based upon the Selfridge Collection of Medici MSS, on deposit in Baker Library, Harvard Graduate School of Business Administration.

[3] The structure of the Florentine banking system will be more fully described by A. P. Usher when he publishes the second volume of his *Early History of Deposit Banking in Mediterranean Europe*. The first volume appeared as Vol. LXXV of the Harvard Economic Studies (Cambridge, 1943). Mr. Usher is in possession of much material on the Florentine banks. Scholars await with interest the results of his research.

of the Venetian *banchi di scritta,* the Genoese Bank of St. George, and the private transfer banks in Barcelona, Bruges, and other commercial centers. As elsewhere, bank failures were not infrequent in Florence. In 1516, there were only three *banchi in mercato* left. One of them, the Da Panzano bank, failed on December 29, 1520.[4] Six years later, when the Imperial troops threatened to besiege Florence, coin became so scarce that the banks suspended specie payments. It is possible that they had been forced to create credit against government loans.[5] At any rate, bank money began to depreciate and the agio on specie soon rose from one half of 1 per cent to 6 per cent. Giovanni Cambi in his chronicle observes that such a thing was a novelty in Florence.[6]

The historic Medici were neither money-changers nor goldsmiths. Their bank was one of those *banchi grossi* or "great banks" which did business "inside" *(dentro).* The office or *scrittoio* of the bank was in the Medici palace. These *banchi grossi* are mentioned with pride by the Florentine chroniclers as one of the main sources of their city's wealth and power. According to the fifteenth-century chronicler Benedetto Dei, there were thirty-three of these banks in 1469 and "they dealt in merchandise and exchange in all parts of the world, wherever there were exchanges or traffic in money."[7] Consequently, the Florentine bankers were traders as well as bankers. They combined foreign trade and dealings in exchange—not petty exchange of foreign for domestic coins, but trade in bills of exchange *(cambium per literas).* To most bankers it was less important than the trade in commodities. Even the Medici, the most prominent firm of merchant bankers in Florence, emphasized trade rather than banking. In 1464, Tommaso Portinari, one of the Medici branch managers, made the statement that "the foundation of the firm's business rests on trade in which most of the capital is employed."[8]

In Florence, as in other Medieval centers—Bruges for example—there

[4] Giovanni Cambi, *Istorie,* III, in *Delizie degli eruditi toscani* (Florence, 1786), XXII, 100, 176.

[5] As was done by the Venetian banks during the war against the Turks.—Frederic C. Lane, "Venetian Bankers, 1496–1533; A Study in the Early Stages of Deposit Banking," *The Journal of Political Economy,* XLV (1937), 205.

[6] Cambi, *Istorie,* III, 299.

[7] "E chambiano e fanno merchantia per tutti i luoghi del mondo, là ove chorrono e chambi e danaro."—Giovanni Francesco Pagnini, *Della decima e di varie altre gravezze imposte dal Comune di Firenze, della moneta e della mercatura dei Fiorentini fino al secolo XVI* (Lisbon-Lucca, 177), II, 275 f.

[8] Armand Grunzweig, *Correspondance de la filiale de Bruges des Medici,* Part I (Brussels, 1931), pp. 129, 131. This is henceforth cited with abbreviated title and page reference only, as Part II has not yet appeared.

was a sharp cleavage between the merchant bankers, whose business interests were international in scope, and the less important *cambiatori* or money-changers, who specialized in local banking. However, all bankers or *tavolieri,* great or small, were required to be members of the Arte del Cambio.[9] On the other hand, the pawnbrokers, who were considered as "manifest usurers," were *ipso facto* excluded from membership in the guild.

Not all Medieval merchants were merchant bankers. A large capital and extensive connections were needed in order to engage successfully in foreign banking. A merchant like Andrea Barbarigo, whose career was recently sketched by Frederic C. Lane, had neither the financial resources nor the connections to set up an international banking business. Such an organization could hardly be built up in one generation. When in 1429 Cosimo succeded his father Giovanni di Bicci, the Medici banking house was already a prospering concern with branches in Venice and *in corte di papa,* at the papal court.[10] The origins of the family could be traced further back in the records of the Calimala and Cambio guilds. However, the period of rapid expansion came during the lifetime of Cosimo. New branches were established in Pisa, Milan, Geneva (moved to Lyons in 1466), Avignon, Bruges, and London. Wherever the Medici had no branch of their own, they had correspondents or agents who would accept or collect the bills of exchange drawn or remitted by their principals. So the Medici were represented by the firm of Filippo Strozzi and Co. in Naples, by Piero del Fede and Co. in Valencia, by Nicolaio d'Ameleto and Antonio Bonafe in Bologna, by Filippo and Federigo Centurioni in Genoa, by Gherardo Bueri—a close relative of Cosimo—in Lübeck, and so forth.[11] All those business firms were Italian and most of them were Florentine. Occasionally the Medici would be represented by a native merchant, as in Cologne where their

[9] The theory of Saverio La Sorsa, *L'Organizzazione dei cambiatori fiorentini* (Ceri, 1904), p. 15, that the merchant bankers were not members of the *Arte del Cambio,* but only of the Calimala and wool guilds is untrue. Averardo de' Medici was a consul of the Arte del Cambio in 1419. Cosimo de' Medici is listed as a member in 1423. Cf. Heinrich Sieveking, *Die Handlungsbücher der Medici* (Sitzungsberichte der Kais. Akademie der Wissenschaften in Wien, Philosophisch-historische Klasse, No. CLI, Vienna, 1905), pp. 4 f.

[10] Heinrich Sieveking, *Aus Genueser Rechnungs- und Steuerbüchern* (Sitzungsberichte der Kais. Akademie der Wissenschaften in Wien, Philosophisch-historische Klasse, No. CLXII, Vienna, 1909), pp. 96 f.; Alberto Ceccherelli, *I Libri di mercatura della Banca Medici e l'applicazione della partita doppia a Firenze nel secolo decimo quarto* (Florence, 1913), p. 43.

[11] Curt S. Gutkind, *Cosimo de' Medici, Pater Patriae, 1389–1464* (Oxford: The Clarendon Press, 1938), p. 192, says erroneously that Edoardo Bueri, brother of Gherardo, was a partner in a Flemish banking house called "de Wale." *Wale* in the Low German of the Middle Ages was simply a designation applied to any person of Latin, French, or Italian origin. "Eduardus de Boeris *de Wale*" means "Edward Bueri, the Italian."

representative was a German named Abel Kalthoff. Cosimo de' Medici did not confine his activity solely to international banking and foreign trade. He had interests also in wool and silk manufacturing, the two principal industries of Florence.

§2. *The Structure of the Medici Firm*

From a legal and structural point of view it is possible to classify the Florentine banking firms according to two different types: those with a centralized, and those with a decentralized, form of organization. The first type was more popular in the thirteenth and fourteenth centuries and was adopted by the Peruzzi, the Bardi, and the Acciaiuoli companies. The failure of these companies explains, perhaps, why this type declined in popularity and gave way to the second type, of which the Medici firm is the best example.

The essential feature of the form of organization exemplified by the Bardi and the Peruzzi companies is that there was only one partnership. It owned the home office in Florence and all the branches abroad. The latter were managed by factors, that is, by agents who received salaries "for the donation of their time" *(per dono del tempo)*. The head of the firm decided whether they ought to be promoted, transferred, retained, or dismissed. Sometimes a partner went abroad in order to serve the company in the capacity of branch manager. In such a case he received a regular salary in addition to the share in the profits to which he was entitled as a partner.[12] A conspicuous example is that of the Florentine chronicler Giovanni Villani, who was a partner in the Peruzzi company and for a time took charge of their office in Bruges.[13]

The capital of the Peruzzi and Bardi companies was divided into shares. In 1331, the capital of the Bardi company was made up of fifty-eight shares: six members of the family held thirty-six and three-quarters shares; the remaining twenty-one and one-quarter shares were owned by five outsiders.[14] In 1312, the Peruzzi company had a capital of £116,000 *a fiorino* or Fl. 80,000 shared by eight members of the

[12] *I Libri di commercio dei Peruzzi,* ed. Armando Sapori (Milan, 1934), pp. 304, 378, and *passim*. Cf. Armando Sapori, "Il personale delle compagnie mercantili del medio evo." *Archivio storico italiano,* Series 7, XXXII (1939), 121–51; *idem,* "Storia interna della compagnia mercantile dei Peruzzi," reprinted from *Archivio storico italiano,* Series 7, XXII (1934), 13, n. 3. Both articles have been reprinted in a volume of collected essays, Armando Sapori, *Studi di storia economica medievale* (2d ed.; Florence: Sansoni, 1946).

[13] Robert Davidsohn, *Forschungen zur Geschichte von Florenz,* III (Berlin, 1901), 96, No. 502.

[14] Armando Sapori, *La Crisi delle compagnie mercantili dei Bardi e dei Peruzzi* (Florence, 1926), p. 249.

Peruzzi family and nine outsiders. In 1331, the outsiders gained control by owning more than half of the capital.[15]

In theory, all partners residing in Florence had a voice in the management. In practice, however, the partners accepted the leadership of one of them. The leading partner inspired enough confidence so that his decisions were usually approved without question. The trouble with this arrangement was that if the leader died there was often no one to take his place. In case of difficulties and losses, quarrels among the partners about policy were likely to make matters worse. Discord among the partners seems to have contributed a great deal to the downfall of the bank of Orlando Bonsignori, a Sienese partnership, and to have played a considerable part in the failure of the Bardi and the Peruzzi companies.[16]

In contrast with these two companies, the Medici banking house was not one partnership but a combination of partnerships. A separate partnership was formed for each of the Medici enterprises: the "bank" or home office in Florence, the branches abroad, and the three industrial establishments in Florence. Each partnership was a separate legal entity or *ragione* and had its own style, its own capital, and its own books. The different branches dealt with each other on the same basis as with outsiders. One branch charged commission to another branch as if both had been parts of different organizations.[17]

The branch managers were not simply factors or employees, as in the case of the Peruzzi, but junior partners who, instead of a salary, received a share of the profits. These managers could not be dismissed, but they could be removed from office by prematurely terminating the partnership, which, according to the articles of association, the Medici had always the right to do.[18] The branch managers had the title "governor" *(governatore)*, whereas the Medici were called "seniors" *(maggiori)*. The use of these terms indicates sufficiently that branch managers had the right to make managerial decisions, but that the Medici who was the head of the firm had the final say in all matters of policy.

In studying the organization of the Medici banking house, one can-

[15] For more details, see Sapori, "Storia interna," pp. 20–23.

[16] Mario Chiaudano, "I Rothschild del Duecento; la Gran Tavola di Orlando Bonsignori," reprinted from *Bullettino Senese di storia patria*, New Series, VI (1935), 17.

[17] Clement Bauer, *Unternehmung und Unternehmungsformen im Spätmittelalter und in der beginnenden Neuzeit* (Jena, 1936), p. 143.

[18] A clause to this effect is inserted both in the partnership agreement of July 25, 1455, relating to the Bruges branch and in that of May 31, 1446, relating to the London branch.—Grunzweig, *Correspondance*, pp. 54, 60; Lewis Einstein, *The Italian Renaissance in England; Studies* (New York: Columbia University Press, 1902), p. 243.

not fail to notice how closely it resembles that of a holding company. The comparison is valid in more than one respect. The Medici controlled the subsidiary partnerships by owning at least 50 per cent of the capital. Besides, there were other means of retaining control. As we shall see below, the partnership agreements carefully circumscribed the powers which were granted to the junior or managing partners. The Medici were also careful to stipulate that they retained the ownership of their trade-mark after the dissolution of a partnership. There was good will attached to their name. This advantage would be lost if they chose to withdraw, as the ambitious Portinari was to learn to his detriment after he broke with the Medici.[19] Today, ownership of stock is not the only means of retaining control. There are trade-marks, patent pools, limited voting rights, interlocking directorates, and other devices.

A lawsuit which was tried before the municipal court of Bruges, in 1455, throws much light on the structure of the Medici business organization. In this case, a Milanese, Damiano Ruffini, brought suit against Tommaso Portinari, as acting manager of the Medici branch in Bruges, for defective packing of nine bales of wool bought by the plaintiff from the Medici branch in London. The defendant pointed out that the bales never belonged to the Bruges branch and that the plaintiff should sue the London branch. To this argument the latter replied that "the Medici branch in Bruges and the one in London were all one company and had the same master." Thereupon, Portinari testified under oath that the two branches were separate partnerships, that the bales of wool had been sold to the plaintiff by the London partnership, and that the Bruges partnership had nothing to do with the sale and should be relieved from all responsibility. The court in its decision dismissed the claim presented by the plaintiff but upheld his right to sue Simone Nori, at that time the manager of the London branch.[20] A similar issue would be raised if a person brought suit in any American court against the Standard Oil of New Jersey for defective merchandise received from the Standard Oil of New York and based his case upon the argument that all Standard Oil companies were controlled by the Rockefellers! Of course, nobody could reasonably expect to win such a lawsuit. But the *Ruffini* v. *Portinari* case goes back to the fifteenth century. At that time commercial law was in an earlier stage of develop-

[19] Grunzweig, *Correspondance*, pp. xxxv. ff.

[20] *Damiano Ruffini* v. *Tommaso Portinari*, Bruges, July 30, 1455, Louis Gilliodts-van Severen, *Cartulaire de l'Estaple*, II (Bruges, 1905), 36 f., No. 958.

ment, and there were presumably no well-established precedents on the issue at stake.

According to a statement prepared for the *catasto* or Florentine property tax in 1458, Cosimo de' Medici was a partner in eleven different enterprises: (1) the "bank" or parent company in Florence managed by Francesco Ingherami; (2) a cloth-manufacturing concern or *bottega d'arte di lana* managed by Andrea Giuntini; (3) another cloth-manufacturing concern managed by Antonio di Taddeo; (4) a silk-manufacturing concern managed by Francesco Berlinghieri and Jacopo Tanagli; (5) the branch in Venice managed by Alessandro Martelli; (6) the branch in Bruges managed by Angelo or Agnolo Tani; (7) the branch in London managed by Simone Nori; (8) the branch in Geneva, styled Amerigo Benci and Francesco Sassetti, managed by Amerigo Benci; (9) the branch in Avignon, styled Francesco Sassetti and Giovanni Zampini, managed by Francesco Baldovini; (10) the branch in Milan managed by Pigello Portinari; (11) a partnership between Cosimo de' Medici and Francesco di Nerone, which was in the process of liquidation. Concerning the branch in Rome, it is stated that Cosimo had no share in the capital, but he probably had some money invested *in deposito*. Apparently, the capital of the branch in Rome was supplied by Cosimo's sons, since the partnership was styled "Piero e Giovanni de' Medici e compagni." In 1458, the managers of the branch in Rome were Roberto Martelli and Lionardo Vernacci. Perhaps it should be emphasized that the name of Medici did not appear in the style of the branches in Avignon and Geneva, although Cosimo owned half or more of the capital.[21]

Even though Cosimo de' Medici was a man full of energy and endowed with unusual managerial ability, he could not possibly manage and supervise everything. Of necessity, he had to delegate power and to rely upon his subordinates. Because of the distance and the slowness of communications, branch managers abroad had to be given a free hand within the frame of the partnership agreement and the instructions with which they had been provided. But what about the "bank" and the wool and silk shops located right in Florence? Even there the head of the firm did not concern himself with details. Whether a particular piece of cloth should be dyed yellow, red, or perhaps purple was a matter for the responsible manager to decide. Cosimo could not be

[21] Sieveking, *Handlungsbücher der Medici*, p. 9; cf. *idem*, *Aus Genueser Rechnungs- und Steuerbüchern*, p. 101.

MARBLE BUST OF FRANCESCO SASSETTI
AT THE AGE OF FORTY-FOUR (1464)

The Workshop of Antonio Rossellino
Museo Nazionale, Florence

bothered with such minor administrative problems. Those were settled by the managers or even by factors or *discepoli* (clerks).

The surviving business records convey the impression that the head of the Medici firm confined himself to making important decisions and to laying down the rules which the managers of the subsidiary partnerships were expected to follow. Cosimo knew how to pick able managers and he kept them well in hand.[22] He insisted that his directions be obeyed to the letter. His prestige was such that nobody dared to disregard his orders. The Bruges manager, Angelo Tani, once incurred Cosimo's wrath by dealing with the Italian firm of pawnbrokers of Bruges and by making an unfavorable settlement after it had failed. Upon learning about these transactions, Cosimo was so incensed that he threatened to terminate the partnership and would have done so if his advisers had not interceded for Tani, who was, after all, an able and cautious manager.[23] For some reason or other, Cosimo distrusted the brilliant, ambitious, and venturesome Tommaso Portinari, then assistant manager of the Bruges branch. He remained a factor until after Cosimo's death, when he was finally admitted as a partner.[24] Later events showed that Cosimo was right in keeping Portinari on a leash. When given authority, he involved the Medici in heavy losses by making excessive loans to Charles the Bold, Duke of Burgundy and ruler of the Low Countries. Portinari himself died in poverty as a result of his mistakes.

Cosimo's successors, Piero and Lorenzo, relaxed their grip on the branch managers. They were given much more leeway than in the lifetime of Cosimo. The results of this change in policy were ultimately disastrous to the prosperity of the Medici banking house.

Historians who have written on the history of Florence or of the Medici have in general overlooked the importance of the role which the manager of the "bank" or main office in Florence played in the administration of all the Medici interests. It appears from the surviving records that his functions were similar to those of the general manager in a modern corporation. During the lifetime of Cosimo, the junior partner

22 Gutkind, *Cosimo*, p. 172. This book on Cosimo contains a few pointed remarks, but it must be used with great caution because of many misstatements of fact and errors in interpretation.

23 Armand Grunzweig, "La Correspondance de la filiale brugeoise des Medici," *Revue belge de philologie et d'histoire*, VI (1927), 725–40.

24 Cosimo de' Medici died on August 1, 1464. Portinari became a junior partner and governor of the Bruges bank when the partnership agreement was renewed on August 6, 1465.—Grunzweig, *Correspondance*, p. xvii.

and manager of the *banco* or main office in Florence was Francesco Ingherami. Either before or, more likely, shortly after Cosimo's death, he retired and was replaced by Francesco Sassetti who became the close business adviser of Piero de' Medici and his son, Lorenzo the Magnificent. Francesco Sassetti had a brilliant record, first as a factor in Avignon and then as junior partner and manager of that branch. Some time before 1453 he was transferred from Avignon to Geneva, but he continued to own a share in the Avignon establishment, presumably as an investing partner. In 1458, Sassetti came to Florence and never returned to his post in Geneva. Because of his outstanding performance as a branch manager, he was probably called upon to assist the aging Francesco Ingherami in the discharge of his duties. At any rate Sassetti gained the confidence of Piero and increased his influence still more under the administration of Lorenzo. From Piero onward, nothing was done without Sassetti's advice.[25]

It was the duty of Francesco Sassetti to examine the reports of the branch managers, to prepare their instructions, to audit the balance sheets of the different branches, to discuss problems with the branch managers when they came to Florence, and to report all matters of major importance to the head of the banking house.[26] Cosimo, as long as he lived, took an active part in the management and did not rely exclusively on the judgment of his advisers. Piero de' Medici, during his short administration, tried to do as much as the poor state of his health permitted. Lorenzo, however, leaned heavily on Sassetti because he was more interested in politics, diplomacy, art, and literature than in business affairs. As those interests absorbed most of Lorenzo's time, Sassetti ceased to receive any guidance through frequent conferences with his master. Probably business decisions were not so carefully weighed as they had been in Cosimo's time.

It is likely that as Sassetti grew older he became the victim of his vanity and self-confidence. Lorenzo's example was apparently contagious, and Sassetti, too, became lax in the discharge of his duties. He probably enjoyed the company of witty humanists more than the reading of dull business reports and the painstaking analysis of uninspiring balance sheets. As a result, the mismanagement of Lionetto de' Rossi, the "gov-

[25] For more details, see Florence Edler de Roover, "Francesco Sassetti and the Downfall of the Medici Banking House," *Bulletin of the Business Historical Society,* XVII (1943), 65–80.

[26] That these were Sassetti's responsibilities is brought out by the letters and the reports of the Bruges branch to the main office in Florence.—Grunzweig, *Correspondance,* pp. 101, 119, 123. Cf. A. Warburg, "Francesco Sassettis letztwillige Verfügung," *Gesammelte Schriften,* I (Leipzig: B. G. Teubner, 1932), 130.

ernor" of the Lyons branch, was not discovered until it was too late to apply effective remedies. If Sassetti had examined the balance sheets with greater care, all sorts of irregularities would not have escaped his attention. He could hardly have failed to notice that the profits of the Lyons branch were grossly overstated, because no adequate provision had been made for bad debts. With regard to the Bruges branch, Sassetti also followed a mistaken policy; he is probably responsible for the recall of Angelo Tani and the appointment in his stead of Tommaso Portinari as manager. When these two disagreed on matters of policy, Sassetti invariably sided with Portinari and overruled Tani, who in vain urged caution and tried to apply the brakes.[27] Instead, Sassetti was instrumental in giving Portinari more and more freedom with each renewal of the partnership agreement.[28] Ultimately this policy had disastrous results.

The fall of the Medici bank engulfed also the fortune of Francesco Sassetti.[29] In Lorenzo's family records Sassetti is given significantly the title "our minister" *(nostro ministro),* that is to say, "our principal executive."[30] It is probable that the supervision of the subsidiaries in Italy and beyond the Alps required considerable attention, so that Francesco Sassetti and his predecessor Francesco Ingherami could devote little time to the management of the *banco* or main office in Florence. They were aided in this task in 1458 by two assistant managers whose names were Giovanni Benci and Tommaso Lapi. The records disclose very little about their duties, but these two men had the power to make out bills of exchange and to obligate the firm.[31] The clerical work which involved little responsibility was entrusted to clerks called *discepoli.* These *discepoli* could not expect any promotion, since executives and branch managers were chosen exclusively from the factors who had been trained for business in one of the branches and knew something about conditions abroad. Sassetti, for example, started his career as a factor in Avignon. Giovanni Benci had probably been in England for

[27] A. Warburg, "Flandrische Kunst und florentinische Frührenaissance," *Gesammelte Schriften,* I, 375, gives an excellent example of Sassetti's partiality.

[28] Sieveking, *Handlungsbücher der Medici,* pp. 48–53.

[29] His last descendants were two brothers. One went to the East Indies in order to retrieve the family fortune. He succeeded in accumulating considerable wealth but died in 1588 of tropical disease. The other sought escape from poverty in writing the history of his family and stressing its antiquity, nobility, and past wealth. It is to him that we owe the story of Francesco Sassetti's rise and fall.—Warburg, "Francesco Sassettis letztwillige Verfügung," *Gesammelte Schriften,* I, 129.

[30] William Roscoe, *The Life of Lorenzo de' Medici* (9th ed.; London, 1847), Appendix x, p. 425.

[31] Sieveking, *Handlungsbücher der Medici,* pp. 22 f.

INTERNAL ORGANIZATION OF THE MEDICI BANK

- **HEAD OF THE FIRM** — COSIMO DE'MEDICI, SUCCEEDED BY PIERO AND BY LORENZO
  - **SILK MANUFACTURING** — ONE PARTNERSHIP
    - **MANAGER IN 1458** — JACOPO TANAGLI
      - SALES — EXPORTERS AND FOREIGN BRANCHES
      - PURCHASES — RAW SILK
      - PRODUCTION
        - THROWING
          - IN A THROWING MILL
        - BOILING
          - COCITORI OR SCOURERS
        - WEAVING
          - WARPERS
          - WEAVERS
        - DYEING
          - TINTORI DI SETA OR DYERS
  - **CLOTH MANUFACTURING** — TWO PARTNERSHIPS
    - **MANAGERS IN 1458** — ANTONIO DI TADDEO AND ANDREA GUNTINI
      - PURCHASES — WOOL FROM IMPORTERS AND BRANCHES
      - SALES OF FINISHED CLOTH — RETAILERS, EXPORTERS, AND BRANCHES
      - PRODUCTION
        - PREPARING THE WOOL
          - WOOLWASHING
          - CAPODIECI
            - BEATERS
            - CLEANERS
          - FATTORE DI PETTINE
            - COMBERS
          - FATTORE DI CARDO
            - CARDERS
        - SPINNING
          - LANINO
            - SPINNERS
          - STAMAIUOLI
            - SPINNERS
        - WEAVING
          - WARPERS
          - WEAVERS
        - FINISHING
          - STRETCHERS
          - BURLERS
          - SCOURERS
          - FULLERS
          - NAPPERS
          - SHEARERS
          - MENDERS
        - DYEING
          - DYERS
            - IN THE WOOL
            - IN THE CLOTH
  - **INTERNATIONAL BANKING AND FOREIGN TRADE**
    - **MINISTRO OR GENERAL MANAGER** — FRANCESCO INGHERAMI LATER FRANCESCO SASSETTI
      - **BRANCHES BEYOND THE ALPS**
        - GENEVA — MOVED TO LYON IN 1466
          - MANAGER — AMERIGO BENCI (1458), LIONETTO DE'ROSSI (1469)
            - SIX FACTORS IN 1469
        - AVIGNON
          - MANAGER — FRANCESCO BALDOVINI (1458), GIOVANNI ZAMPINI
            - FOUR FACTORS IN 1469
        - BRUGES
          - MANAGER — ANGELO TANI (1456–65), TOMMASO PORTINARI (1465–1481)
            - ASSISTANT MANAGER — ANTONIO DI BERNARDO DE'MEDICI
              - SIX FACTORS IN 1466
                - WOOL AND CLOTH TRADE
                  - CRISTOFANO SPINI
                - SILK TRADE
                - BANKING AND FOREIGN TRADE
                - OTHER CLERICAL WORK
                - BOOKKEEPING
                - LETTER BOOK AND ERRANDS
        - LONDON
          - MANAGER — SIMONE NORI (14[illegible]–1465), GHERARDO CA[illegible]IGIANI (1465–147[illegible])
            - SEVERAL FACTORS
      - **BANCO OR HOME OFFICE** — IN FLORENCE
        - TWO ASSISTANT MANAGERS — TOMMASO LAPI AND GIOVANNI BENCI, LATER FRANCESCO NORI (SLAIN IN 1478)
          - SEVERAL CLERKS OR DISCEPOLI
      - **BRANCHES IN ITALY**
        - VENICE
          - MANAGER — ALESSANDRO MARTELLI (1458)
            - FACTORS
        - ROME
          - MANAGERS — ROBERTO MARTELLI AND LEONARDO VERNACCI (1458), AFTER 1464 GIOVANNI TORNABUONI
            - FOREIGN BANKING
            - FOREIGN TRADE
            - FISCAL AGENTS OF THE PAPACY
        - MILAN
          - MANAGER — PIGELLO PORTINARI
            - FACTORS

a number of years before he was called to an important post in the central administration.[32] Promotions were sometimes slow. Tommaso Portinari was forty years old before he became a branch manager and had served the firm for more than twenty-five years as a factor in Bruges.[33] In 1478, at the time of the Pazzi conspiracy, one of the assistant managers was apparently Francesco di Antonio Nori, who was slain in the fray that followed the murder of Giuliano di Piero de' Medici, Lorenzo's brother, during High Mass in the cathedral of Santa Maria del Fiore (April 26, 1478). According to Sassetti's private account book, Francesco Nori had been the manager of the Geneva and Lyons branch until 1468, when he was expelled from France for incurring the displeasure of Louis XI.

§3. *The Central Administration and the Branches*

The relations between the main office and the branches outside Florence can be studied from the partnership agreements concluded between the Medici and their branch managers, from the written instructions with which the latter were provided upon leaving Florence, and from the correspondence exchanged between the main office and the branches. Branch managers usually came to Florence every two or three years in order to report on business conditions and administrative problems. During these visits branch managers were given oral instructions and they conferred frequently with the *maggiori,* or senior partners, and with the general manager.[34] Unfortunately no minutes of these meetings were kept. All we know is that they took place and that important decisions were often reached after informal discussion of managerial problems.

Partnership agreements are documents of fundamental importance because they determine not only the division of capital and profits, but also the obligations of the partners toward each other. According to the Medici partnership agreements the senior partners retained all the

[32] This statement is based on the fact that Benci was a partner of the Medici company in London.—Einstein, *Italian Renaissance,* p. 242. Former branch managers usually were retained as partners; for example, Angelo Tani, who had been the branch manager in Bruges from 1455 to 1465, still had a share in the capital of this branch when it was liquidated in 1481.—Grunzweig, *Correspondance,* p. xxxiv.

[33] He was about twelve years old when he came to Bruges in 1437 as a *giovane* or office boy. At that time the Bruges branch was managed by his cousin Bernardo Portinari, a son of Giovanni Portinari, who was in charge of the Medici branch in Venice from 1418 to 1430 or thereabouts.—Grunzweig, *Correspondance,* p. xiii. The Portinari were descended from a brother of the Beatrice made famous by Dante in his *Divine Comedy.*

[34] Portinari to Cosimo de' Medici, March 28, 1464, and May 14, 1464.—Grunzweig, *Correspondance,* pp. 110, 130.

power, but the junior partner assumed all the burden of managing the common undertaking. All his actions were subject to the approval of the senior partners who had the right to terminate the partnership at any time, if they were displeased. The main purpose of the articles of association was to define the duties of the managing partner and to restrict his powers. Let us take as an example the partnership agreement of July 25, 1455, concerning the Bruges subsidiary of the Medici bank.[35]

There were three parties to this contract: (1) Piero and Giovanni de' Medici, the two sons of Cosimo, who was still living, and Pierfrancesco de' Medici, the son of Lorenzo, Cosimo's deceased brother; (2) Gierozzo de' Pigli, the former manager; (3) Angelo Tani, the new manager. Although Cosimo himself is not mentioned in the contract, we should remember that appearances are sometimes deceiving. As *pater familias,* he was the real power behind his sons and his nephew. Gierozzo de' Pigli was not merely a dormant partner; he was consulted in certain cases by Cosimo de' Medici, who was *de facto,* if not *de jure,* the senior partner. Angelo Tani, the junior partner, was to assume the "government" of the company for four years beginning March 25, 1456, and ending March 24, 1460 (N.S.). The purpose of the company or partnership was to trade "in exchange and merchandise in the city of Bruges in Flanders."

According to article one, the style of the company was to be "Piero di Cosimo de' Medici, Gierozzo de' Pigli and Co." The capital was set at £3,000 groat, Flemish money, to be supplied as follows: £1,900 groat or more than half by the senior partners, members of the Medici family; £600 groat by Gierozzo de' Pigli; and £500 groat by Angelo Tani (art. 2). Next it was stipulated that the profits were to be divided in the proportion of 12*s.* to the pound or 60 per cent to the Medici, 4*s.* to the pound or 20 per cent to Gierozzo de' Pigli, and 4*s.* to the pound or 20 per cent to Angelo Tani. The latter, who supplied only one sixth of the capital, received one fifth of the profits. It was customary to give the manager a larger share of the profits both as a reward for his services and as an inducement to make profits. No capital or profits could be taken out of the company during the duration of the contract with the exception that Tani, the junior partner, was allowed to withdraw £20 groat a year for his living expenses. Losses, "may God forbid," were to be shared in the same proportion as the profits (art. 3).

[35] The Italian text of this partnership agreement was published with a summary in French by Grunzweig (*Correspondance,* pp. 53–63) and republished without any summary by Gutkind (*Cosimo,* pp. 308–12).

ANGELO DI JACOPO TANI, MANAGER OF THE BRUGES BRANCH,
AND HIS WIFE, CATERINA TANAGLI

Hans Memling
Formerly in the Marienkirche, Danzig

BRUGES BRANCH
DIVISION OF CAPITAL AND ALLOCATION OF THE PROFITS
ACCORDING TO THE PARTNERSHIP AGREEMENTS
FROM 1455 TO 1471 *

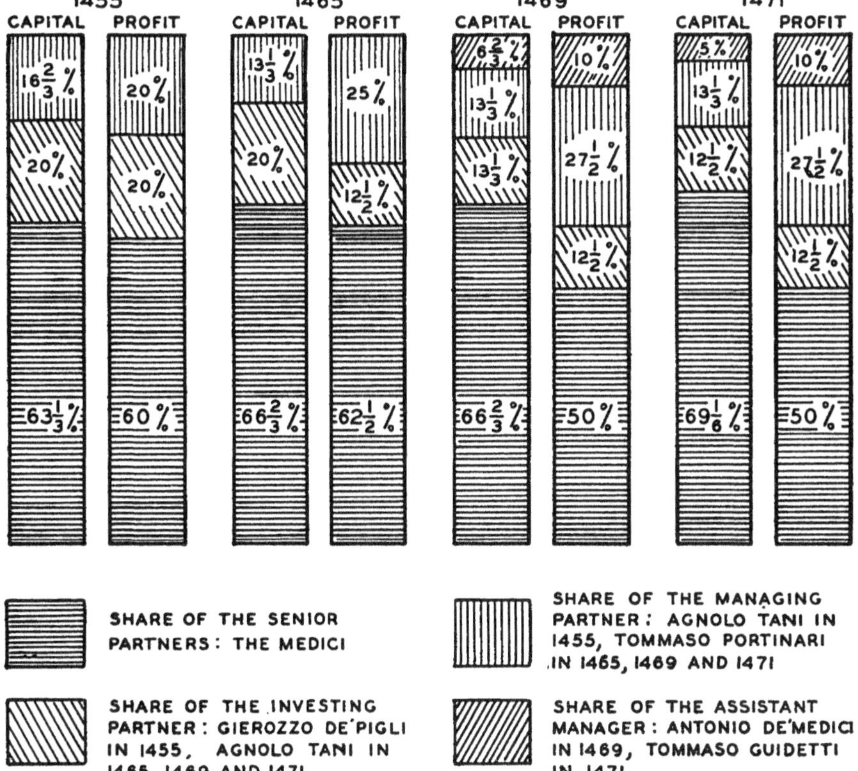

* SOURCE SIEVEKING, DIE HANDLUNGSBÜCHER DER MEDICI PP 48–52

The contract required that Tani reside in Bruges and confine his activities "to lawful trade and to licit and honorable exchange transactions" in accordance with instructions given by the Medici and Gierozzo de' Pigli (art. 2).[36] Tani was allowed, however, to visit the fairs of Antwerp and Bergen-op-Zoom and to make business trips to London, Calais, or Middelburg, if necessary (art. 12).[37]

[36] The phrase "licit and honorable exchange transactions" obviously refers to exchange transactions which were permissible according to the church.

[37] The fairs of Antwerp and Bergen-op-Zoom grew steadily in importance during the fifteenth century. These fairs were regularly attended by the manager of the Medici branch in Bruges or by members of his staff.—Grunzweig, *Correspondance*, pp. 135 f. Bergen-op-Zoom, not to be confused with Bergen in Norway or Bergen (Flemish for Mons) in Hainaut, is a Dutch town on the Scheldt estuary some twenty miles north of Antwerp. I wonder where Gutkind found support for the statement (*Cosimo*, p. 191) that the Medici had a branch or

Tani had permission to extend credit and to deliver money by exchange to merchants and artificers only. Even then he was to consider their credit standing and reputation. Loans to princes were consequently ruled out, a point which should be kept in mind in view of later developments. Under no conditions was the branch manager allowed to sell foreign exchange on credit to lords spiritual or temporal. In other words he could not issue letters of credit either on Rome or on any other place, unless they had been paid for in advance. Any violation of these rules was subject to a penalty of £25 groat for each offense (art. 4). The contract further forbade Tani to make any commitments for other merchants (for instance, to stand surety) or to send goods on consignment to other than Medici companies (art. 5). Tani also promised that he would do no business for himself, either directly or indirectly, whether in Bruges or elsewhere. Any breach of this promise entailed a heavy penalty of £50 groat and confiscation of the profits for the benefit of the partnership. Should there be losses, then Tani would have to bear those himself (art. 6).

Every year the senior partners were to receive a copy of the balance sheet as of March 24, the last day of the year according to the style of the Incarnation. However, Tani was bound to supply a copy of the balance sheet at any time, if so requested by the senior partners. At the end of the contract, he could be called to Florence in order to report in person on his management and to help expedite the final settlement of accounts (art. 8). As we know from the correspondence, these provisions were actually carried out. Each year on March 24, the bookkeeper of the Bruges branch closed the books and drew up the balance sheet. A copy of the latter was sent at the first opportunity to Francesco Ingherami, or later to Francesco Sassetti, in Florence.[38]

It was further provided that Tani could not buy wool or cloth, either English or Flemish, for more than £600 groat in a given year without the written permission of the senior partners (art. 13). All shipments by sea had to be properly insured for their full value, except that Tani could venture, uninsured, up to £60 groat, but not more in one bottom, if goods were shipped aboard the Florentine or the Venetian galleys. He was free to insure or not to insure those goods which were transported overland, but no risks were to be run for more than £300 groat at one time (art. 14). As we know from other sources, goods traveling

permanent establishment in Antwerp. I have found nothing concerning the existence of an Antwerp branch.

[38] For example, the balance as of March 24, 1464, was sent from Bruges to Florence on May 14, 1464.—Grunzweig, *Correspondance*, pp. 129, 130 f.

overland were not usually insured, although examples of such insurance are found in the fifteenth century. As for the galleys, they were considered so safe that many merchants did not deem it necessary to take out insurance. They preferred to limit their risks by dividing their shipments among several bottoms.[39]

The partnership agreements of 1455 contained a few other provisions of minor importance. For example, Tani, the junior partner, was allowed neither to gamble nor to entertain a woman in his quarters (art. 7). He was not supposed to accept any gifts above the value of one pound groat (art. 16). The purpose of this clause was evidently to prevent corruption. If Tani violated the local laws and ordinances, he had to bear the consequences of such infringements (art. 18). He was not even empowered to hire factors or office boys without the written permission of his partners (art. 10). It is doubtful whether such permission was ever granted. As a rule factors and *giovani* or office boys were sent out to the branches by the main office in Florence, and the branch managers had no voice in the matter. Another provision forbade Tani to underwrite insurance or to make wagers (art. 15).

The expiration of the contract or its premature termination did not free Tani from all obligations. He had to stay in Bruges for another six months in order to wind up the company's business. During this time no new commitments were to be made and everything possible was to be done in order to speed up the liquidation of the assets, the collection of the outstanding claims, and the payment of the current liabilities. After completion of this process the capital was to be refunded to the partners and the profits, if any, were to be divided among them (art. 19). In practice, however, things worked out somewhat differently. Capital and accumulated profits were not refunded in cash, but were written to the credit of the partners, either in capital or current account, in the books of the succeeding partnership. Usually the latter also took over some of the assets and assumed some of the liabilities. The transition from one partnership to another was effected without any interruption in the ordinary course of business. The only danger was that of mixing up the accounts of the two partnerships. In order to avoid confusion, the bookkeeper worked for a time with two sets of books, those of the old, and those of the new, partnership. In the ledger of the old partnership an account was opened to the *ragione nuova* or new partnership. Similarly, an account was created for the *ragione vecchia* or

[39] Frederic C. Lane, *Venetian Ships and Shipbuilders of the Renaissance* (Baltimore: The Johns Hopkins Press, 1934), p. 26.

old partnership in the books of its successor. These two accounts were reciprocal and, if correctly kept, canceled each other.

In connection with the liquidation of the partnership, the agreement further provided that the living quarters, the office, and the warehouse (*casa e fondaco*) were to remain the property of the Medici (art. 9).[40] After winding up the business, the books and papers were to be sent from Bruges to Florence and were to remain there in the custody of the senior partners. Tani, the junior partner, would have access to the archives, if need be. The senior partners also undertook to settle the few contingent liabilities which might still be in dispute after paying off the other debts. Funds were to be set aside for this purpose.

Any differences arising from the partnership agreement were to be submitted to the Court of the Mercanzia in Florence. Tani as manager could bring suit against third parties or defend suits brought against the firm before any jurisdiction, especially before the *loya* or municipal court of Bruges and the law courts of London, Venice, and Genoa.[41]

The partnership agreement which has been analyzed here varies only in unimportant details from a similar contract concluded in 1446 between the Medici and Gierozzo de' Pigli, at that time manager of the London branch.[42] It is, therefore, safe to consider the partnership agreement of 1455 as representative of similar agreements which were entered into by the Medici and by other Italian merchant-bankers.

The agreement of 1455, as we have shown, placed many restrictions upon the freedom of the managing partner. Some of these safeguards were removed in later agreements, probably under the influence of Francesco Sassetti. As a result of this change in policy, the managing partner was given much more freedom and some of the more stringent provisions were considerably relaxed. Sassetti made the fatal mistake of lifting the ban on loans to princes or governments. When the partnership agreement concerning the Bruges branch was renewed in 1471, permission was granted to Tommaso Portinari, then local manager, to

[40] The real estate in Bruges apparently belonged privately to the senior partners and the partnership paid rent for the use of this property. In 1466, Portinari bought a palatial mansion in Bruges, the Hôtel Bladelin, for Piero de' Medici.—Grunzweig, *Correspondance,* p. xxv. The building was large enough to accommodate the offices of the Bruges branch, the manager and his family, and probably the members of the staff. The partnership paid a rental of £30 groat a year. Not more than £20 groat a year were to be spent on upkeep and improvements—Sieveking, *Handlungsbücher der Medici,* p. 52.

[41] The records of the municipal court in Bruges refer frequently to Angelo Tani and his successor Tommaso Portinari as plaintiffs or defendants in suits of law. *Loya* is not an Italian word, but was commonly used in Italian records to designate the municipal court of Bruges, which was called in French *la loi de Bruges* and in Flemish *de wet van Brugge.*

[42] Einstein, *Italian Renaissance,* pp. 242–45.

lend up to £6,000 groat to Charles the Bold, Duke of Burgundy and ruler of the Low Countries. This sum was twice the firm's entire capital. The debt, moreover, was allowed to run over the limit of £6,000 groat. By 1478, about the time of the Pazzi conspiracy, the government of the Low Countries owed £9,500 groat to the Medici.[43] Although Lorenzo the Magnificent and Sassetti were well aware of the dangers involved in such loans, they gave their consent, the agreement states, "because of the good qualities of this illustrious prince [Charles the Bold] and because of the many favors received from him through his friendship for Tommaso Portinari."[44] The latter had become the Duke's councilor and wielded great influence at the Burgundian court in the Low Countries. The loans, however, did not turn out to be a good investment. Charles the Bold suffered defeat in a war against the Swiss and fell in battle at the siege of Nancy in 1477. His death left the government of the Low Countries in desperate straits, without army, without allies, without treasury, without authority, and with the French on the doorstep ready for an invasion. In order to save what he had already lent, Tommaso Portinari was forced to throw good money after bad and to grant additional credits to Charles the Bold's impecunious son-in-law, Archduke Maximilian of Austria. Only part of the loans was eventually repaid, and that very slowly.[45]

Portinari also obtained a free hand in another matter. He secured permission to operate the two Burgundian galleys built in Pisa, in 1464, for Philip the Good, Duke of Burgundy. Piero, in 1469, had ordered the liquidation of the Medici interests in this shipping venture.[46] But the partnership agreement of 1471, concluded after Piero's death, allowed Portinari to keep the Burgundian galleys.[47] After a few successful voyages from Bruges to Pisa and even to Constantinople, that ill-starred venture came abruptly to a disastrous end: one of the two galleys was captured in 1473, by a Danzig privateer; the other was wrecked in a

[43] Georges Bigwood, *Le Régime juridique et économique du commerce de l'argent dans la Belgique du moyen âge* (Mémoires in-8 de l'Académie Royale de Belgique, Series 2, No. XIV, Brusssels, 1922), I, 663. Bigwood states that the debt amounted to £57,000 Artois, at 40 groats to a pound, which is equivalent to £9,500 groat, at 240 groats to a pound.

[44] Sieveking, *Handlungsbücher der Medici*, pp. 50, 52.

[45] The liquidation of the loans dragged on until 1500, when a crown jewel, the fleur-de-lis of Burgundy, held in pledge by Portinari, was finally released. The toll of Gravelines near Calais assigned to Portinari in 1478 was still in his control in 1495.—Bigwood, *Régime*, I, 663. As the years passed, the toll yielded less and less revenue because of the decline of the wool staple at Calais.—Grunzweig, *Correspondance*, pp. xxxvi-xxxix.

[46] Sieveking, *Handlungsbücher der Medici*, pp. 50, 62.

[47] *Ibid*, p. 52.

storm the following year.[48] The capture of the one galley gave rise to diplomatic complications and lawsuits which lasted for more than twenty-five years.

The provisions of the partnership agreements were supplemented by written instructions which the branch managers received when they left Florence to go to their posts. These instructions were more specific than the articles of association and called attention to the pitfalls that were to be avoided in the conduct of business and the extension of credit. The only instructions still extant in the Medici archives in Florence are those given to Gierozzo de' Pigli when he started out from Florence, in 1446, to assume the management of the London branch.[49] His journey was mapped out for him by Cosimo de' Medici, the senior partner. He was to travel by way of Milan and Geneva, where the Medici had branches, thence through Burgundy to Bruges, and from there to London. In Milan he was to gather further information about the credit standing of several concerns dealing with England. The next stopping place was Geneva, where the branch manager was absent on business. There Gierozzo de' Pigli was expected to watch the behavior of the factors and to report on their doings. If something was wrong, he was instructed to straighten the matter out; his orders would be obeyed. In Bruges, the manager Bernardo Portinari was also absent, but Pigli would meet the two principal factors, Simone Nori and Tommaso Portinari.[50] They would be useful in giving additional data about business conditions in England. Here, too, Pigli was expected to keep his eyes open and to report on what he saw. Once in London, he would find Angelo Tani, his main assistant (the same person who later became manager of the Bruges branch). Tani, in Cosimo's opinion, was best fitted to keep the books and to attend to the correspondence. Another factor, Gherardo Canigiani, according to the instructions, was probably satisfactory as a cashier, while a third factor, who had mastered English, was perhaps

[48] Evidence that the Burgundian galleys went as far as Constantinople is found in the account book of a Florentine merchant, Bernardo Cambi, who underwrote insurance on them for voyages from Flanders to Pisa and Constantinople. See Florence Edler de Roover, "A Prize of War: A Painting of Fifteenth Century Merchants," *Bulletin of the Business Historical Society,* XIX (1945), 3–11; *idem,* "Early Examples of Marine Insurance," *The Journal of Economic History,* V (1945), 191, 194.

[49] Einstein, *Italian Renaissance,* pp. 245–49.

[50] Bernardo Portinari, a cousin of Tommaso, was manager of the Bruges branch from 1437 to 1450 or thereabouts. He was replaced by Gierozzo de' Pigli who was transferred from London to Bruges. Pigli's successors were Angelo Tani (1455–65) and Tommaso Portinari (1465–80). In the latter year, the Medici withdrew from Bruges. The London branch was managed by Gierozzo de' Pigli (1446–50), by Simone Nori (1450–60), and by Giovanni de' Bardi (1460–66). Gherardo Canigiani never became managing partner of the London branch.

most useful in going about the city on the firm's affairs. However, Gierozzo de' Pigli had the necessary authority to distribute the work as he thought best. No credit was to be given, and no bill of exchange purchased without his knowledge or permission. In places where the Medici had branches, Pigli was to deal with them in preference to other firms. In particular, he was urged to work closely with the Bruges branch. In places where the Medici had no branches, Pigli was to select his correspondents among the merchants who had a reputation of reliability and good service. If he was asked to be their agent in London, he was to reciprocate by giving them satisfaction in every respect. Consignments of wool and cloth could be sent to the Medici houses in Florence, Rome, Milan, and Venice, and to the companies controlled by the Medici in Avignon, Geneva, and Pisa.

The instructions further urged Pigli to be cautious in making new contacts. At Naples there was probably no one with whom he could safely deal; at Rome there were the Pazzi, whose credit was good, and several other firms which could be trusted for limited amounts; at Florence there were also several concerns, such as the Serristori and the Rucellai, the solvency of which was beyond question. Cosimo professed that he knew little about Venetian merchants.[51] He therefore advised Pigli to be cautious in dealing with them. The instructions mentioned several firms of good repute in Genoa, Avignon, Barcelona, and Valencia. Pigli was to have no business relations with either Brittany or Gascony, but he could accept consignments of wine from those regions as

[51] It is hard to believe that Cosimo was really ignorant of business conditions in Venice, where the firm maintained a branch office and where he, himself, while in exile, had resided about twelve years earlier (1433–34). The explanation of Cosimo's warning to Pigli against dealing with Venetians must be sought in the sphere of politics rather than that of business. In 1446, relations between Florence and Venice had ceased to be friendly and had become increasingly strained because of Cosimo's support of Francesco Sforza, who was bidding for the succession of the Visconti in Milan. Cosimo feared that Venice might conquer Lombardy, an event which would have upset the balance of power in Italy.—E. W. Nelson, "The Origins of Modern Balance-of-Power Politics," *Medievalia et Humanistica,* I (1943), 124–42. The relations between the two republics went from bad to worse, and open warfare broke out in 1451 with Florence and Milan allied against Venice which received the support of the king of Naples. As soon as war was declared, the Florentine merchants were expelled from Venetian territory and their property was seized. Cosimo, foreseeing the course of events, had withdrawn most of his capital from Venice to Milan where he had opened a new branch (*ca.* 1450). Peace was not concluded until 1454. It is understandable that Cosimo did not want his partners to lend to Venetian merchants, when there was danger that such credits would be frozen or impounded in the event of war. This episode is an example of the way in which the business policy of the Medici was sometimes affected by political considerations. Cf. Ferdinand Schevill, *History of Florence from the Founding of the City through the Renaissance* (New York: Harcourt, Brace and Company, 1936), pp. 360–61; F. T. Perrens, *The History of Florence under the Domination of Cosimo, Piero, Lorenzo de' Medicis, 1434–1492* (London, 1892), pp. 64–123, esp. p. 103 concerning the confiscation of Florentine property.

long as it was a matter of no importance. He was to have nothing to do with Catalan merchants. Regarding Englishmen who traded with Flanders, Pigli was to use his judgment in granting them credit or in taking their bills of exchange. In buying goods, he was to be careful that he did not pay more than the merchandise was worth.

Cosimo de' Medici and his son Giovanni hoped that Pigli would enjoy the favor of the King and Queen (Henry VI and Margaret of Anjou). If necessary, a letter of recommendation from King René, Margaret's father, would be procured.[52]

In short, as this outline of Cosimo's instructions shows, Gierozzo de' Pigli was expected to follow a policy of caution in the extension of credit, in the selection of agents, and in the purchase of commodities. Diversification was not enough. Cosimo apparently feared the cumulative effect of many small mistakes as much as the dangers arising from an inadequate division of risks.

Correspondence was the only means by which the senior partners and the main office of the Medici bank kept in contact with the branches, since the slowness of transportation prevented frequent consultations with the branch managers. Only a small fraction of this voluminous correspondence has come down to us and is available in print. This published material is made up exclusively of letters sent to Florence by the Bruges and London branches. There seem to have been two kinds of letters: the *lettere di compagnia* or business letters and the *lettere private* or confidential private letters.[53] The *lettere di compagnia* were addressed to the firm or *banco* in Florence. They dealt chiefly with current business affairs: notices concerning bills drawn or remitted, information concerning shipments or the safe arrival of consignments, advices concerning debits and credits, and similar details. The rates of exchange quoted in London or Bruges were usually given at the end. Since the *lettere di compagnia* did not deal with confidential and important subjects, their contents did not have to be concealed. These letters were passed on to the bookkeeper, who needed them to make the necessary entries in the books, and to the other members of the staff, who handled bills of exchange or took care of shipments, purchases, and sales.

The *lettere private* were not addressed to the firm, but personally to Cosimo or other members of the Medici family. A few *lettere private* are congratulatory messages regarding family events or deal with the

[52] René of Anjou, Count of Provence, was pretender to the crown of Naples.
[53] Grunzweig, *Correspondance*, pp. xlv-xlix.

Courtesy of the Metropolitan Museum of Art, New York

TOMMASO PORTINARI, MANAGER OF THE BRUGES BRANCH AND COUNCILOR TO THE DUKE OF BURGUNDY, AND HIS WIFE, MARIA BANDINI-BARONCELLI

Hans Memling

The Altman Collection, The Metropolitan Museum of Art, New York

purchase of tapestries for members of the Medici family. Those letters are of little importance to history. The same is not true of the other *lettere private* wherein the writers discuss business prospects, political events, important problems of management, and the financial condition of the branches. Since the Medici were rulers as well as merchant bankers, they were much interested in the course of political events which might affect either their business or their foreign policy. Furthermore, it should not be overlooked that men like Portinari, who was councilor to the duke of Burgundy, moved in court circles and took part in important diplomatic negotiations. They had access to inside information and served the Medici not only as business managers but also as informants and diplomatic agents. In dealing with the Medici, one should remember that business decisions sometimes suffered from the dictates of political necessity. This is especially true of the policy of the Medici with regard to government loans.

§4. *The Management of the Branches*

Thus far the discussion has been confined to the organization of the *banco* in Florence and to the relations between the main office in Florence and the branches. Let us now take a glimpse into the daily life of one of the branches or *fondachi*. Since our information is nearly complete for the Bruges branch, it will be chosen as a typical example of the organization of all the other branches. In 1466, the staff of the Bruges branch included Tommaso Portinari, the branch manager, five factors, and two *giovani* or office boys. The five factors were Antonio di Bernardo de' Medici, Cristofano Spini, Carlo Cavalcanti, Tommaso Guidetti, and Adoardo Canigiani. The two *giovani* were Folco Portinari, a nephew of the branch manager, and Antonio Tornabuoni, a nephew of Piero de' Medici, who had married Lucrezia Tornabuoni.[54]

Tommaso Portinari had recently been admitted as a partner when the partnership agreement was renewed on August 6, 1465. He received no salary, but was entitled to one fourth of the profits, although he owned only £400 groat out of a total capital of £3,000 groat, that is, two fifteenths of the total. In official documents Portinari called himself "governor and partner of the society of Piero de' Medici and Co."[55] As

[54] *Ibid*, p. xxvi.

[55] In a Latin document dated January 21, 1468 (N.S.), Portinari called himself *socius et gubernator societatis egregii domini Petri de Medicis ac sociorum*. This document was first published by Adolf Gottlob, "Zwei 'Instrumenta cambii' zu Uebermittelung von Ablassgeld (1468)," *Westdeutsche Zeitschrift für Geschichte und Kunst*, XXIX (1910), 208, and later translated into English by William E. Lunt, *Papal Revenues in the Middle Ages* (Records of

a partner, he needed no power of attorney to obligate the company or to represent it in court. Antonio di Bernardo de' Medici was the assistant manager and became acting manager whenever Tommaso Portinari was absent for a period of time. Since Antonio was a factor and not a partner, he could not represent the firm in court or in deeds without either a general or a special power of attorney.[56] In 1469, Antonio de' Medici was admitted to the firm as a junior partner, while Portinari himself became a senior partner and the equal of the Medici. According to the contract of 1469, the share of Antonio in the capital was one fifteenth and his share in the profits, one tenth.

Next in rank to Antonio de' Medici came Cristofano Spini. He was in charge of the purchases of wool and cloth, which required the keeping of special records. Carlo Cavalcanti was entrusted with the sale of silk cloth at the court. This job had been given to him because of his fluency in French and his attractive appearance and manners.[57] French —not Flemish, the popular tongue—was the language of the Burgundian court and of fashionable society in Medieval Bruges. It requires little imagination to picture Carlo Cavalcanti, dressed like a *damoiseau* in a handsome doublet, using his most persuasive charms to sell his silks to the fair ladies at the court of Burgundy. Adoardo Canigiani did not have so pleasant an assignment; he was the bookkeeper. A surviving fragment of the ledger of the Bruges branch shows that the books were carefully kept and that the double entry method was in use.[58] No spe-

---

Civilization, No. XIX, New York: Columbia University Press, 1934), II, 469–74. Lunt translates *socius et gubernator* as "colleague and governor" instead of "partner and governor" (meaning "manager"). "Colleague," to the best of my knowledge, is not a term used in business. *Procuratore* would have been better translated as "proxy" or "attorney" than by "proctor." The expression £ *grossorum monete Flandrie* should have been translated as "£ groat of Flemish money" and not as "£ of the large money of Flanders," which is meaningless. The standard expression in English for *indulgentiarum plenissarum* is "plenary indulgences" and not "fullest indulgences."

[56] A factor could not represent a firm in public instruments without power of attorney. A good example is given in the document quoted in note 55, which is a deed wherein Cristofano Spini acknowledged the receipt of a sum of £1,773 10*s.* 3*d.* groat as attorney for, and in the name of, Tommaso Portinari *(procuratore et ex nomine)*. Spini gave acquittance in virtue of a power of attorney drawn up in Bruges on January 16, 1468 (N.S.).

[57] Gutkind's statement (*Cosimo,* p. 183) that Cavalcanti was "an expert on French connexions" is confusing. There was no "French" court and nobility in Bruges. "French-speaking" instead of "French" would have been less misleading.

[58] The assertions by Gutkind (*Cosimo,* p. 174) that double-entry bookkeeping had not yet been introduced and that few facts are known about the accounting system of the Medici bank are absolutely wrong. Gutkind is apparently repeating the misstatements of Otto Meltzing, *Das Bankhaus der Medici und seine Vorläufer* (Jena, 1906), p. 83. The studies of Ceccherelli and Sieveking listed by Mr. Gutkind in his bibliography prove the contrary. The Medici kept their accounts with great accuracy. Furthermore, balance sheets were comprehensive and included all assets and liabilities.

cific information is available about the functions of Tommaso Guidetti, but it is likely that he was the cashier and perhaps also handled the bills of exchange. Antonio Tornabuoni, the *giovane* who had just arrived from Italy, was probably set to work on the letter book in which all outgoing letters were copied before being dispatched.

Personnel problems were by no means unknown in the Middle Ages. As we have seen, factors were sent from Florence and were not appointed by the manager. This system had its inconveniences. A youngster by the name of Corbinelli, who had been sent to Bruges by the senior partners, was so dull that he was shipped back to Italy after a short trial. Antonio di Bernardo de' Medici, the assistant manager, was another liability. He had a disagreeable disposition and was thoroughly disliked by the other members of the staff.[59] Even Portinari held him in little esteem. But family ties were strong in the Middle Ages and the Renaissance. Although Antonio was only a distant relative of the senior partners, he was protected by the fact that he belonged to the same family and bore the name Medici. The other factors were greatly disappointed when they learned, in 1469, that Antonio had been raised above them to the rank of junior partner and presumptive successor to Tommaso Portinari. After a quarrel involving Cristofano Spini, all the factors threatened to resign if Antonio de' Medici remained in Bruges. As a result of these difficulties, the partnership agreement of 1469 was terminated before it had expired. A new agreement was made on May 12, 1471. Antonio de' Medici was dropped. In his place Tommaso Guidetti became junior partner and assistant manager. He had a share of one twentieth in the capital and of one tenth in the profits. Portinari, the manager, was entitled to 27.5 per cent of the profits, but his share in the capital was more than twice that of Guidetti.[60]

In 1470, according to the chronicle of Benedetto Dei, the Bruges branch had a staff of eight including Tommaso Portinari and Antonio di Bernardo de' Medici, respectively manager and assistant manager, and six factors: Cristofano Spini, Tommaso Guidetti, Lorenzo Tanini, Folco Portinari, Antonio Corsi, and Antonio Tornabuoni. The handsome Carlo Cavalcanti had left the service of the Medici, but was still in Bruges, probably selling silks to his fair customers at the court of Burgundy. The Bruges branch of the Pazzi, the principal competitors of the Medici, also had a staff of eight members including Francesco Nasi, Francesco Capponi, Berto Tiero, Pierantonio Bandini-Baroncelli,

[59] Grunzweig, *Correspondance,* pp. xxv-xxvii.

[60] Sieveking, *Handlungsbücher der Medici,* p. 52.

Bartolomeo Nasi, Niccolò Capponi, Dionigi Nasi, and Filippi Buciegli.[61]

§5. *The Management of the Industrial Establishments in Florence*

Besides the bank and its branches in Italy and beyond the Alps, the Medici controlled and partly owned three industrial establishments in Florence: one *bottega di seta* or silk shop and two *botteghe di lana* or cloth-manufacturing establishments. Except for the papal alum mines in Tolfa, the Medici had no direct interest in any manufacturing or mining enterprise outside of Florence.[62]

With regard to these three industrial establishments in Florence, the Medici followed the same policy as with their other undertakings. Since it was impossible to direct and to decide everything, Cosimo de' Medici and his successors entered into partnership with men who had expert knowledge of the technical processes of making silk fabrics or woolen cloth and who took charge of the management. Emphasis was on production and quality rather than on trade. The output was sold either locally to exporters or consigned to the Medici's own branches abroad. As we have already seen, the Burgundian court in Bruges was a buyer of silk stuffs produced by the *bottega di seta* owned by the Medici.[63] Large quantities of the finest cloth that came out of the two Medici shops were sold by the Milan branch to the court of the Sforza and to prominent Milanese citizens.[64]

The Florentine silk and woolen industries were both organized on the basis of the putting-out or "wholesale handicraft" system. The work, instead of being done in a factory or a central workshop, was carried on very largely in the homes of the workers. They used their own tools, but the materials were provided by the master manufacturer or industrial entrepreneur. Since the manufacturing process, especially

[61] Pagnini, *Della decima,* II, 304–5.

[62] I question very much Gutkind's statement (*Cosimo,* p. 183) that "cloth made from English wool was also produced by the [Medici] firm itself in Flanders." The Medici made contracts with tapestry makers concerning special orders, but did not try to make either cloth or tapestries in their own establishment in Flanders. I have not found a shred of evidence to prove that the Medici branch in Bruges "bought the wool, spun, and wove it."—*Ibid,* p. 202.

[63] Grunzweig, *Correspondance,* p. xxii.

[64] Curzo Mazzi, "La Compagnia mercantile di Piero e Giovanni di Cosimo de' Medici in Milano nel 1459," *Rivista delle biblioteche e degli archivi,* XVIII (1907), 17–31. For example, the cloth account contains several items relating to pieces of cloth sent to Milan by *i nostri lanaioli di Firenze,* that is, by our cloth manufacturers in Florence. The Milan branch also sold English and Flemish cloth received on consignment from the Medici company in Bruges.—*Ibid.,* p. 24. The text should read: "E dì 14 d'ottobre £316 per tanti ragionamo qui £17 s.15 d.6 di grossi [not *di guadagno*] di Bruggia mettendo a grossi [not *a guadagno*] 54½ per ducato." The money of Bruges was the pound groat called *lira di grossi* in Italian.

in the woolen industry, involved many steps, it was quite a problem to keep track of the materials which continuously flowed in and out of the manufacturer's shop. Wages were on a piece-rate basis rather than by the hour or by the day because the employer could control output but not time. The maintenance of quality was another important problem which required constant vigilance on the part of the manager. Careless work caused complaints from customers and lowered the price at which the finished product could be sold. And the Medici sold mainly to people who demanded high quality but were less particular about price.

In 1458, Cosimo de' Medici controlled two *botteghe di lana* or cloth-making establishments: one was managed by Antonio di Taddeo and the other by Andrea Giuntini. The first was known under the style of Piero de' Medici, Cosimo's elder son, and the second, under the style of Giovanni de' Medici, Cosimo's younger son.[65] These two shops already existed in 1432.[66] The total capital of each of them was Fl. 5,000 or less.[67] According to Cosimo's declaration, in 1458, for the *catasto* or Florentine property tax, the Medici had an investment of Fl. 2,500 in one shop and Fl. 2,100 in the other shop. As no articles of association are available, it is impossible to know how the profits were divided.

The organization of the Florentine woolen industry is well known through the studies of Doren and the business records of another branch of the Medici family.[68] The manufacturing process included in all twenty-six different steps, but they can be grouped together in five major processes: the preparatory process, spinning, weaving, dyeing, and finishing.[69] Most of the steps in the preparatory process—sorting, cleansing, combing, and carding—were performed in the shop of the Medici under the supervision of industrial factors or overseers. Most of the other steps were performed either in the homes of the workers or in outside establishments, some of them belonging to the wool guild. The

65 Sieveking, *Handlungsbücher der Medici*, p. 9.

66 Giuseppe Canestrini, *La Scienza e l'arte di stato; ordinamenti economici: della finanza, parte 1, l'imposte sulla ricchezza mobile e immobile* (Florence, 1862), p. 157; Richard Ehrenberg, *Das Zeitalter der Fugger* (3d ed.; Jena, 1922), I, 47.

67 Gutkind (*Cosimo*, p. 194) states that, in 1432, the capital was Fl. 10,000 for each of the two shops. This figure is certainly erroneous and is apparently based upon the assumption that the tax rate was one half of 1 per cent. We do not know the rate of the levy of 1432, but it was certainly higher than one half of 1 per cent.

68 Alfred Doren, *Studien aus der Florentiner Wirtschaftsgeschichte:* Vol. I, *Die Florentiner Wollentuchindustrie* (Stuttgart, 1901); Florence Edler [de Roover], *Glossary of Mediaeval Terms of Business, Italian Series, 1200–1600* (Cambridge: The Mediaeval Academy of America, 1934), especially the appendixes, pp. 335–426; Raymond de Roover, "A Florentine Firm of Cloth Manufacturers," *Speculum*, XVI (1941), 3–33.

69 Edler, *Glossary*, pp. 324–29, gives a complete list of these steps.

spinning, for example, was done by country women to whom industrial factors brought the wool and from whom they collected the yarn.

The giving out of the materials to so many different workers complicated the problems of control and required the keeping of elaborate records in order to prevent the waste of materials and to figure out the remuneration of the industrial factors and the wage earners. The job of manager was by no means a sinecure. It involved a great deal of responsibility since the senior partners could not possibly check on everything. They interfered only when something went seriously wrong. As in foreign trade and banking, the judicious choice of an efficient and honest manager was the key to success or failure. The Medici were probably able to secure the services of good managers. Antonio di Taddeo, mentioned in 1458 as manager of one of the two *botteghe di lana,* was still running this establishment in 1470, twelve years later.[70] He must have given the Medici satisfactory service in order to retain his position.

The manufacture of silk cloth involved fewer steps than the production of woolen cloth. The silk manufacturers usually bought reeled silk that had already received a slight twist. The reeled silk was probably sent by the Medici to a water-driven throwing mill where several strands were twisted together and retwisted to form strong threads. Boiling, dyeing, warping, and weaving followed. All these steps were performed outside the Medici shop, either in the homes or in special establishments. Unlike woolen cloth, silk fabric did not require any finishing when it came from the loom. It is likely that quality was even more important in the silk than in the woolen industry.[71]

Although some sixteenth-century business records concerning the Florentine silk industry are extant, they have not yet been studied, so that the organization of the silk establishments is less well known than the setup of a typical firm in the woolen industry. Running a silk establishment or *bottega di seta* was in any case more than one man could do. The Medici had both a manager and an assistant manager to do the job. According to the partnership agreement of 1437, the capital invested in the silk shop was Fl. 5,000 of which Fl. 4,200 were provided by Cosimo de' Medici and Fl. 800 by Francesco Berlinghieri, the manager. A third partner, Jacopo di Birago, presumably the assistant manager, did not put any money into the business, but was nevertheless entitled to a share of the profits. These were to be divided as though

[70] Sieveking, *Aus Genueser Rechnungs- und Steuerbüchern,* p. 101.

[71] I am indebted for this information to my wife, Florence Edler de Roover, who has made a careful study of the Lucchese silk industry. Cf. Edler, *Glossary,* pp. 330–31.

Cosimo had invested only Fl. 3,000 instead of Fl. 4,200; Francesco, Fl. 1,400; and Jacopo, Fl. 600; that is, in the following proportions: Cosimo 60 per cent, Francesco 28 per cent, and Jacopo 12 per cent.[72] By 1458 a man named Jacopo Tanagli had become assistant manager. At that time the capital invested by the Medici was only Fl. 3,300. In 1469, the senior partners were Lorenzo the Magnificent and Pierfrancesco de' Medici, his first cousin; Francesco Berlinghieri was apparently dead and had been succeeeded as manager by his son, Berlinghieri di Francesco Berlinghieri; Jacopo Tanagli was still a junior partner.[73]

As this survey shows, the slowness of communications and the intricacy of the manufacturing processes in the textile industry forced the head of the firm to delegate considerable powers to the branch managers. He had neither the time nor the opportunity to busy himself with inconsequential details. Even important matters were decided by the local managers. General policy alone was determined from above. For purposes of control much reliance was placed on frequent reports, written or oral, but the absence of a satisfactory system of inspection and of internal check was a serious weakness of the Medici business organization. Perhaps too much depended upon the careful choosing of responsible managers. Serious mistakes made by managers could rarely be caught in time to prevent irreparable damage.

The interests of the Medici in international banking and foreign trade by far outweighed their interests in manufacturing. According to the figures for the *catasto* of 1458, an aggregate of Fl. 28,800 was invested in the capital *(corpo)* of the bank at Florence and in the branches abroad.[74] This total does not include the share of the Medici in the capital of the branch in Rome. Furthermore, the total does not include the Medici's share in accrued profits which were usually allowed to accumulate over several years before a distribution took place. The Medici, in addition to their share in the capital of their banking

72 Sieveking, *Handlungsbücher der Medici,* p. 47.

73 Sieveking, *Aus Genueser Rechnungs- und Steuerbüchern,* p. 101.

74 The figure of Fl. 28,800 is made up as follows:

Florence	Fl. 5,600
Venice	6,000
Bruges	3,500
London	4,800
Geneva	3,500
Avignon	2,400
Milan	3,000
Total	Fl. 28,800

and trading enterprises, usually invested in them considerable amounts under the form of interest-bearing deposits. These items, too, are not included in the total of Fl. 28,800, so that the aggregate investment in trade and in banking by far exceeded this amount. On the other hand, only Fl. 7,900 were invested in manufacturing.[75] Probably this amount is too low and should be slightly increased. In any case, there can be no doubt that the Medici were chiefly merchant bankers and not industrial entrepreneurs.

[75] The figure of Fl. 7,900 is made up as follows:

1. Share of the Medici in the capital of the silk establishment	Fl.	3,300
2. Share in the capital of first woolen-cloth establishment		2,500
3. Share in the capital of second woolen-cloth establishment		2,100
	Fl.	7,900

TOMMASO PORTINARI AND HIS WIFE
(Portinari is in the scales; his wife is in front of him)

Hans Memling
Detail from the Central Panel of the Triptych, "The Last Judgment"
Formerly in the Marienkirche, Danzig

Part II

FINANCIAL AND COMMERCIAL OPERATIONS

ACCORDING to the articles of association, the purpose of the Medici partnerships, of the *banco* in Florence, and of the branches abroad, was "to deal in exchange and in merchandise with the help of God and good fortune." When we ask just what is meant by dealings in exchange and in merchandise, we are led to examine how the Medici raised the funds with which they operated, to study their role as fiscal agents of the papacy and lessees of the Tolfa alum mines, to consider the technique they used in international banking, and to look into the reasons for their failure. The Medici did not innovate in international banking, they followed existing business practice; but their records are an extremely valuable source of information, if only for the sake of comparison. Let us begin by finding out what is meant by dealings in exchange and then tackle the other problems.

§1. *Banking and Exchange Transactions*

Up to the middle of the seventeenth century, "banker" and "exchanger" were synonymous terms. *Fare il banco* and *fare il cambio* ("to engage in banking" and "to deal in exchange") were one and the same thing. Exchange, of course, refers to the trade in bills of exchange and not to the petty exchange of one currency for another. Strangely enough, the mechanism of the Medieval money market has been generally misunderstood. One source of error is the widespread belief that in the Middle Ages bills of exchange were discounted as they are today. As a matter of fact there is not a single instance of a bill being discounted in the business records of the Medici or in those of other merchant bankers that I have examined. The modern practice was introduced in England about the middle of the seventeenth century, when the London goldsmiths began to discount domestic or "inland" bills. In the Middle Ages, all bills were foreign bills and always involved an exchange transaction, whence the name, bill of "exchange."[1]

[1] Raymond de Roover, "Early Accounting Problems of Foreign Exchange," *The Accounting Review*, XIX (1944), 403. R. D. Richards, *The Early History of Banking in England* (London: P. S. King and Son, 1929), pp. 43–47, 236–37, mentions the development of inland bills but fails to stress the most important point, namely, that "inland" bills were discountable in seventeenth-century England, while "outland" bills were not. Richards also failed to explain of what "the business of exchange" really consisted.

Today a banker who discounts a bill knows his profit in advance, since interest is deducted at once from the face value of the bill. The borrower receives credit only for the face value minus the discount. Such a transaction would have been unlawful in the Middle Ages. It was usury to take a certain gain on a *mutuum,* that is, on a straight loan without "adventure of the principal."[2] A *mutuum* was always *gratis et amore,* that is, free of charge. It would be wrong to assume that Medieval merchants disregarded and openly defied the canons of the church. The grip of the church on the minds of the faithful was very strong. Medieval merchants accepted the canonist doctrine as businessmen of later ages accepted mercantilism and the laissez-faire theories of Adam Smith and Ricardo.[3] The Medici would have vigorously denied that they were manifest usurers. Perhaps they might have conceded that some of their transactions were dubious or on the border line between legitimate and illegitimate business.

It is clear from the business records of the Medici and of other merchant bankers that bills were not discounted but were bought and sold at prices which were determined by the rate of exchange. The purchase of a bill involved both an exchange and a credit transaction, since the buyer or lender, usually called "deliverer" *(datore),* by giving a sum of money to a borrower or "taker" *(prenditore),* received in return an instrument which was payable at a future date and, of course, in a different place and in a different kind of currency.[4] As a rule, exchange dealings were confined to time bills. Because of the slowness of communications, even sight drafts were in effect time bills. Most Medieval bills, however, were payable at usance. Usance was three months between Italy and London, two months between Italy and Bruges, and one month between Bruges and London or Paris.

Today the profit of the banker is certain, in the sense that interest is computed on a percentage basis. In the Middle Ages, however, his profit was uncertain, since it depended upon the unpredictable swing of the exchange rates.[5] Usually the lender gained and the borrower lost,

[2] The principle that "an exchange transaction is not a straight loan" (*cambium non est mutuum*) was generally accepted by scholastic writers.

[3] Cf. Armando Sapori, *Mercatores* (German trans., Milan: Garzanti, 1942), chap. v, "Der Kaufmann und die Religion," pp. 127–48, esp. pp. 144 ff.

[4] The word *prenditore* may cause confusion because its meaning changed in the seventeenth century. From then onward the payee or beneficiary of a bill is called *prenditore.* Prior to the seventeenth century, however, *prenditore* referred to the person who received the value and made out the bill, that is, the drawer.

[5] Even in the seventeenth century, the Dutch writer J. Phoonsen pointed out that the uncertainty of gain was an essential feature of the exchange contract.—*Les Loix et les coutumes du change des principales places de l'Europe* (Amsterdam, 1715), p. 3. This contract was

but the reverse could and did happen if the exchange rates for one reason or another were momentarily out of gear. Occasionally the banker or deliverer neither gained nor lost but just managed to break even. In the eyes of the churchmen this uncertainty of the lender's profit justified exchange transactions. Careful analysis reveals, however, that "pure" interest was hidden in the exchange rates.[6]

In the most important centers of Medieval Europe, there existed a bill market. The buying and selling of bills was done through brokers, and prices, that is, the exchange rates, depended upon the conditions of supply and demand prevailing in the money market.[7]

The mechanism of the Medieval money market is not easy to explain or to understand, because exchange transactions in the past were so very different from what they are today. Each bill involved two markets: the one where it was issued and the one where it was payable. There were four different kinds of bills: (1) those drawn by a principal on his agent (2) or the reverse, and (3) those remitted by a principal to his agent (4) or the reverse. The words "principal" and "agent" have here a strictly technical meaning. For each single exchange transaction one had to determine who was acting as principal and who was acting as agent. The "principal" was the individual or the firm who initiated an exchange transaction and assumed the risk of any loss. The "agent" was the person or firm who carried out the orders from a foreign principal. The main office of the Medici bank in Florence could act either as agent or as principal of any of its branches. For example, the main office was acting as principal if it decided to draw on the Bruges branch, to remit to the Bruges branch, or ordered the Bruges branch either to draw or to remit. On the other hand, the main office was acting as agent if it drew, remitted, collected, or paid bills of exchange upon instructions from the Bruges branch.

Relations between the different branches of the Medici bank were the same with regard to bills between any two of them. One branch could

---

defined as follows: "Le change des marchands est un *négoce* d'argent que les marchands exercent d'une place sur une autre, ou d'une foire sur une autre, pour un *gain incertain et casuel,* et ce change est appelé par excellence change simple [italics mine]." Cf. Tommaso Buoninsegni, *Dei cambi, trattato risolutissimo et utilissimo* (Florence, 1573), fol. 5ᵛ.

[6] An exposition of the theory of interest in exchange will be found in my study, "What is Dry Exchange? A Contribution to the Study of English Mercantilism," *The Journal of Political Economy,* LII (1944), 250–66.

[7] It is untrue that "bill-broking does not appear before the eighteenth century."—Curt S. Gutkind, *Cosimo de' Medici, Pater Patriae, 1389–1464* (Oxford: The Clarendon Press, 1938), p. 281. The merchant manuals of the Middle Ages give the tariff of brokerage charges, and the account books of Medieval merchants often give the names of the brokers through whom bills were negotiated.

act either as principal or as agent for another branch. Relations between the Medici bank and outsiders were on exactly the same basis: the Medici sometimes acted as agents for other firms and sometimes as their principals.

The principal opened to his agent a *Nostro* account in which were recorded all exchange transactions carried out by the agent "for our account" (*per nostro conto,* that is, for the "principal's" account). *Nostro* accounts usually represented balances held by correspondents abroad in their capacity of agents and in the currency of the foreign country. *Nostro* accounts were therefore kept in both local and foreign currency. When a *Nostro* account balanced in foreign currency but not in local currency, the difference represented either a profit or a loss arising from exchange transactions. Such differences were transferred to Profit and Loss.

In contrast to *Nostro* accounts, *Vostro* accounts were opened by bankers in their capacity of agents to foreign correspondents in their capacity of principals. Such accounts were used to record all bills which were bought, sold, paid, or collected for others, that is "for their account" *(per loro conto)* or "for your account" *(per vostro conto). Vostro* accounts represented balances held in local currency for foreign principals. Unlike the *Nostro* accounts, *Vostro* accounts had only one extension column, for the local currency, and did not require adjustment for exchange differences. *Vostro* accounts, on the other hand, frequently included charges for commission, brokerage, and consular fees.[8]

The Medici dealt extensively in exchange. The surviving fragments of their account books contain countless items relating to bills of exchange. Their offices in different places acted sometimes as principals and sometimes as agents for each other or for outsiders. Each office or branch of the Medici bank opened a *Nostro* account to the main office as agent and a *Vostro* account to the main office as principal, and did likewise for the other branches. For example, in the ledger of the Medici branch at Bruges, there is both a *Nostro* and a *Vostro* account open to the Medici firm at Venice: one is called *Chosimo de' Medici e compagni di Vinegia, per nostro chonto* and the other, *Chosimo de' Medici e compagni di Vinegia, per loro chonto.*[9]

To understand the mechanism of Medieval banking, it is essential to

[8] A detailed description of the mechanism of *Nostro* and *Vostro* accounts is given in my study, "Early Accounting Problems of Foreign Exchange," *The Accounting Review,* XIX, 381–407. See Appendixes IV and V, pp. 73–77 and 78–81.

[9] Florence, Archivio di Stato, Mediceo avanti il Principato, filza 134, no. 2, Fragment of a ledger belonging to the Bruges branch, 1441, fols. 241, 250. (Hereafter cited as A.S.F., Ledger of Medici Bruges branch.)

grasp the difference between *Nostro* and *Vostro* accounts. An example is perhaps the best way of making this difference clear. Let us suppose that the Medici branch in Bruges remitted a bill to the Medici branch in Venice. Either the latter's *Nostro* or *Vostro* account could be charged for this remittance, depending upon which branch was principal and which was agent in the given transaction. The *Nostro* account would be charged with the remittance if the Medici of Bruges had bought the bill with their own funds, but the bill would be written to the debit of the *Vostro* account if the purchase was made upon orders from Venice and with funds belonging to the Medici in that city. The two transactions were dissimilar in yet another respect. In the first case the Medici in Bruges would have increased their holdings in Venetian ducats. In the second case, however, the Medici in Venice would have reduced the balance, in Flemish currency, standing to their credit in Bruges.

For the sake of clarity, it may be well to repeat that the purchase of a foreign bill involved an extension of credit as well as the acquisition of a claim on balances abroad. Medieval merchant bankers who made loans to customers by buying their bills had to operate on at least two markets and sometimes on three. A banker who had bought a bill received credit abroad. The most advantageous use of such a credit was often the purchase of a second bill in order to bring home the money invested in the first bill. A transaction of this sort was called *cambium et recambium* and involved two bills instead of one: one for the exchange—from Venice to Bruges, for example—and one for the reexchange—from Bruges to Venice. If the Medici in Venice bought a bill on Bruges, they would receive credit in Bruges at the end of two months. But their profit as bankers would remain indeterminate until they bought in Bruges a bill on Venice with the proceeds of the first bill. They could also draw on their balance in Bruges—by selling a bill on Bruges in Venice—but a draft was likely to be less profitable than a remittance.

The fragment of the ledger of the Medici branch in Bruges contains many entries referring to transactions of this kind. Unfortunately, debit and credit entries rarely match in date or in amount, and it is rather difficult to pick out a real case that will serve for the purpose of illustration. At any rate, I have been able to find one case that will do.

Around July 15, 1441, the Medici of Venice bought a bill on Bruges at the rate of 54½ groats per Venetian ducat.[10] Two months later, when

[10] Exchange rates were quoted in so many groats, Flemish currency, per Venetian ducat or per florin, both in Bruges and in Venice or Florence, respectively.

the bill matured, they received in Bruges 54½ groats for each ducat. With the proceeds of this bill the Bruges branch, acting as agent for the Venice branch, bought a bill on Venice, payable at the end of two months, at the rate of 51½ groats per ducat. The Medici of Venice thus made a profit of 3 groats on each ducat over a period of four months, since they received 54½ groats and paid only 51½ groats. If the exchange rate in Bruges had been 54½ groats instead of 51½ per ducat, the Medici of Venice would have been broken even because they would have paid and received the same number of groats for each ducat. If the exchange rate in Bruges had been higher than 54½ groats, the Medici of Venice would have incurred a loss instead of making a profit.

Instead of waiting for a remittance from the Medici branch in Bruges, the Medici of Venice might have resold their Flemish exchange by drawing a bill on Bruges. In such a case, they would have gained with a falling exchange and lost with a rising exchange. They had bought Flemish currency at 54½ groats per ducat. If they had resold it at 55 groats, they would have lost one-half groat per ducat, since the Medici of Bruges would have received 54½ groats per ducat from the remittance but would have been bound to pay out 55 groats per ducat for the draft. On the other hand, a fall of the exchange from 54½ groats to 54 groats would have resulted in a profit of one-half groat.

Conditions of equilibrium required that the exchange rate of the ducat always be higher in Venice than in Bruges. Such was the usual case but it sometimes happened that the exchange rates misbehaved. An interesting example is given in the extant fragment of the ledger of the Medici branch in Bruges. Apparently, the Medici of Venice, early in April 1441, expected a rise of the exchange with Bruges within the subsequent few weeks, and they decided to sell a time draft payable in Flemish currency to one Piero Horco residing in Venice. This sale was made at the rate of 51½ groats per ducat. The Medici of Venice immediately received the face value of the draft or 370 ducats. At the end of the customary period of two months, the Medici of Bruges credited Horco's account with £79 *7s.* *11d.* groat, or 370 times 51½ groats, in Flemish currency. This entry did not complete the transaction, because the Medici of Venice had apparently agreed to repurchase the Flemish currency at the rate prevailing in Bruges at the time that the draft reached maturity. Since the exchange in Bruges was then at 52 groats, the £79 *7s.* *11d.* groat were reconverted into ducats at that rate, and the Bruges branch of the Medici wrote to the Venetian branch that they owed Piero Horco only 366 ducats and 10½ *grossi* instead of 370 ducats. The Medici of Venice had thus made a profit of 3 ducats and 13½ *grossi* and, besides, had enjoyed the use of 370 ducats during four months. The profit arose from the difference of one-half groat in the rate of the ducat: 51½ groats in Venice and 52 groats in Bruges.

Usually the lender gained and the borrower lost, but this rule was not true in every single case. In this example, the Medici, who were the borrowers, made a profit at the expense of a lender who made a wrong forecast. According to the ledger of the Bruges branch, the ducat rose from 51½ groats to 54½ groats in Venice and from 49 or 50 groats to 52½ groats in Bruges during April, May, and June 1441. As long as the exchange was rising, it was advantageous for Venice to draw on Bruges and for Bruges to remit to Venice. The opposite was true of a falling exchange, which made it profitable for Venice to remit and for Bruges to draw.

Changes et vents
Changent souvent.

Winds and exchange
Often change.

This saying was common among merchant bankers operating in the money market. The fact that commercial credit and exchange were welded together introduced a speculative element into the banking business by making profits depend upon the fickle behavior of the exchange rates.[11] It is not surprising that bankers watched exchange fluctuations very closely and tried to forecast the trends in the money market. The Medici received regular reports from their correspondents about the state of the money market in different places. Their policy was apparently the same as that of other merchant bankers, that is, they tried to be deliverers where the money market was "tight," money was "dear," and bills were "cheap," and to be takers where money was

[11] The banker usually gained but he lost occasionally when the money market was not in equilibrium. This point is clearly stated by Lodovico Guicciardini in his famous description of exchange transactions on the Antwerp bourse, found in his *Descrittione di tutti i Paesi Bassi* (Antwerp, 1567). In the better known French translation (by F. de Belleforest, 1582), the relevant passage is as follows: ". . . . et toutefoys cest usage de change ordinairement est non seulement tolérable, mais commode et de grand prouffit, et ne peut (suyvant que disent les Théologiens), estant pratiqué deuëment, porter nom de gain injuste: d'autant que le plus souvent on y gaigne peu et encor avec grand hasard et peril, et telle foys on y perd du fondz et principal de la chose."—R. H. Tawney and Eileen Power, eds., *Tudor Economic Documents* (London: Longmans, Green and Company, 1924), III, 160.

plentiful and bills sold at a good price.[12] The game was risky, however. As communications were slow, conditions in foreign money markets were apt to have changed completely by the time letters reached their destination. Much reliance had to be placed therefore upon the judgment of the correspondents with whom the Medici kept their balances.

Exchange transactions had one advantage: it was easy to spread risks by making no commitments beyond a certain sum and by being careful in picking out reliable takers. Although bills were purchased outright and not discounted, the deliverer always had the right of recourse against the taker or drawer if the drawee failed to pay a bill at maturity.

Takers were generally merchants, such as Andrea Barbarigo, who had little capital and borrowed by selling bills. Powerful merchant bankers, such as the Medici, the Pazzi, and the Strozzi, were usually lenders, but they occasionally became borrowers if they needed to replenish their foreign balances or if they expected the price of bills to fall.[13] The Medici operated on the exchange not only with their own funds but also with the funds of depositors, mostly noblemen and other persons of wealth. Thus landowners and other people without any connection with business participated indirectly in the financing of foreign trade.

Although the Medici professed to deal only in lawful exchange, several clear cases of dry exchange are found in the ledger of the Bruges branch.[14] Dry exchange was a spurious exchange transaction which was actually a cloak for a straight loan. For example, the Medici of Venice would lend money to a borrower who did not have any foreign exchange to sell but who would be told to make out a bill on the Medici of Bruges payable to the same. When this bill arrived at maturity after two months, the Medici of Bruges would draw another bill on the same Venetian borrower for the value received from themselves and in favor of the Medici in Venice. The borrower had the use of the money lent during a period of four months, while the bills traveled from Venice to Bruges and thence back to Venice. He did not pay any fixed interest

[12] Tightness in the money market usually corresponded to a rising exchange in Venice and Florence and to a falling exchange in Bruges. When the tension lessened, the exchange tended to fall in Venice and Florence, but to rise in Bruges.

[13] A fall in the price of bills corresponded to a rising exchange in Venice, since the taker promised to pay more in Flemish currency for each ducat received in Venice, and to a falling exchange in Bruges, since the taker there received less in Flemish currency for the promise to pay one ducat in Venice.

[14] A.S.F., Ledger of Medici Bruges branch, fol. 231 (account of Antonio di Niccolò del Conte). See Appendix VI, pp. 82–83.

on the loan, but the exchange rates determined how much the lender would get as a profit or, occasionally, how much he would lose on the transaction.[15] Whether or not dry exchange was permissible was perhaps still a doubtful matter in the fifteenth century. One of the leading authorities on business ethics, San Antonino, Archbishop of Florence, was of the opinion that dry exchange was usury *(usura est)* because a profit was made on a *mutuum* or straight loan.[16] More than a hundred years later dry exchange was officially condemned as usurious by a decretal promulgated by Pius V on February 5, 1571 (N.S.), in the sixth year of his pontificate.[17]

Medieval bills of exchange were holograph documents, that is, they were written entirely in the hand of the maker.[18] Not all the members of the Medici staff had the right to make out bills. In the main office in Florence only the general manager (Francesco Ingherami) and the two assistant managers (Giovanni Benci and Tommaso Lapi) had this power, according to an entry in some kind of a bills-payable and bills-receivable register kept by the Medici.[19] Another register of the same sort contains a list of the correspondents whose hand *(mano),* not just signature, had to be honored.[20] There are examples of a drawee refusing to accept a bill because he was unable to identify the handwriting of the maker.[21]

15 In the case of three loans made to Antonio di Niccolò del Conte, the Medici just broke even in one instance and made a profit in the other two instances.—R. de Roover, "What is Dry Exchange?" *The Journal of Political Economy,* LII, 263 f.

16 The text of San Antonino is quoted by Amintore Fanfani, *Le Origini dello spirito capitalistico in Italia* (Milan, 1933), p. 112.

17 Joannes Baptista Lupus, *De usuris et commerciis illicitis* (Venice, 1582), pp. 109 f., gives the text of the decretal which is cited or referred to by a great many other authors.

18 Abbott Payson Usher, *The Early History of Deposit Banking in Mediterranean Europe* (Harvard Economic Studies, No. lxxv, Cambridge, 1943), I, 76 f.

19 This register, dated 1455, is described by Heinrich Sieveking, *Die Handlungsbücher der Medici* (Sitzungsberichte der Kais. Akademie der Wissenschaften in Wien, Philosophisch-historische Klasse, No. CLI, Vienna, 1905), p. 23, who reads into the text that Ingherami, Benci, and Lapi were three messengers who rode from one city to another delivering bills of exchange! He comments on the inadequacy of the postal service. In reality, the text lists the names of the manager and assistant managers in Florence who had the power to make out bills of exchange and against whose "handwriting" foreign correspondents could validly pay. For example, the firm Piero and Giovanni de' Medici at Rome was expected to honor any bills issued by the bank in Florence and written in the hand of Giovanni Benci, Francesco Ingherami, or Tommaso Lapi ("A Roma, a Piero e Giovanni de' Medici e Compagnia di corte, scrivemo che per noi ànno a dare compimento . . . . per mano di Giovanni Benci, per mano di Francesco Ingherami, per mano di Tomaso Lapi").—Florence, Archivio di Stato, Mediceo avanti il Principato, filza 134, no. 3, fol. 42.

20 The Italian text is *per cui mano aremo a dare chonpimento.*—Sieveking, *Handlungsbücher der Medici,* p. 22. Sieveking believes that this passage also refers to messengers who came to Florence to present bills of exchange. The meaning of the text is entirely different.

21 Prato, Tuscany, Datini Archives, no. 854, Letter of the firm Giovanni Orlandini and Piero Benizi and Co. in Bruges to Francesco di Marco e Andrea di Bonanno in Genoa, dated

It would be useless to search the Medici ledgers for an account called "Interest Income" or something equivalent. Profits from banking originated in differences in exchange rates, not in fixed interest charges. Such profits on exchange transactions were kept separate from trade profits and written to the credit of an account entitled *Avanzi e Disavanzi di Bancho* ("Profit and Loss on Banking").[22] The same practice was followed by other merchant bankers.[23]

As an adjunct to the exchange business, the Medici branches sold letters of credit, chiefly on Rome, to travelers, pilgrims, ecclesiastics, and students, either going to Italy or residing there. As we have seen, such letters of credit were paid for in advance. The extant fragment of a ledger of the Bruges branch contains two or three examples of transactions of this sort. For instance, two letters of credit for a total of 500 ducats *di camera* were sold, in 1441, to Master Anselm Fabri, dean of the Church of Our Lady of Antwerp, who resided in Rome because of his office at the Curia.[24]

§2. *Commercial Transactions*

The organization of international trade in the days of the Medici differed as much from that of the present day as did the banking system. The two main characteristics of Medieval trade were venture trading and lack of specialization. Both were the outcome of the conditions which prevailed in the Middle Ages and for a long time thereafter, up to the late eighteenth century.[25] As a rule, Medieval merchants were merchant adventurers who sought safety against high risks in the diversification of their ventures.[26] This diversification is well expressed by Antonio in Shakespeare's *Merchant of Venice* (Act I, scene 1):

> Believe me no, I thank my fortune for it,
> My ventures are not in one bottom trusted,
> Nor to one place; nor is my whole estate
> Upon the fortune of this present year:
> Therefore my merchandise makes me not sad.

September 3, 1400: ". . . . voi no gli avete promessi perchè la lettera non era di mano di chi suole fare quelle del chanbio."

[22] Sieveking, *Handlungsbücher der Medici, p.* 35.

[23] R. de Roover, "Early Accounting Problems of Foreign Exchange," *The Accounting Review,* XIX, pp. 383, 394–98.

[24] A.S.F., Ledger of Medici Bruges branch, fol. 245. Cf. Canon Floris Prims, "Heer Anselmus Fabri, onze tiende deken (1415–1449)," *Antwerpiensa* (Antwerp, 1938), XI, 19–26.

[25] N. S. B. Gras, *Business and Capitalism: An Introduction to Business History* (New York: F. S. Crofts and Company, 1939), p. 120.

[26] The English merchant adventurers later formed a regulated company called the "Company of Merchant Adventurers." The term "merchant adventurers" does not apply only to the members of this company.

The Medici were no exception to the general rule. They also diversified their risks by dealing in a great many commodities, but the mainstay of their business was trade in certain staple products and luxury articles, such as wool, cloth, silk, alum, dyestuffs, spices, olive oil, and citrus fruits, for which there was a steady demand in the principal commercial centers. Risks were further spread by entering into joint ventures or "anonymous partnerships" with other merchants.[27] In many cases the Medici refused to take any risks at all and were satisfied to sell consignments on a commission basis.[28] In some instances commodities were bought for others "on their account" and at their risk. For example, in 1441 the Medici branch in Venice bought common ginger for the Medici branch in Bruges. In the latter's books the cost of the ginger in Venetian ducats was written to the credit of the *Nostro* account of the Venetian branch.[29] This entry shows clearly that the Medici branch in Venice was acting simply as agent for the Medici branch in Bruges. The invoice was evidently made out in ducats and payable in the same currency. The Medici branch in Venice did not run any risks, not even the risk of adverse exchange fluctuations.

Today, in the overseas trade, the buyer usually seeks out the seller, and goods are not shipped without being sold. This is especially true of heavy equipment and manufactured products which are made to order according to the specifications of foreign buyers. In the Middle Ages, however, the consignment trade was dominant because buyers wanted to inspect personally the quality of the goods offered for sale and did not usually place orders in foreign countries. Because of the prevalence of this practice, it was up to the seller to find an outlet for his wares. Most Medieval merchants were adventurers in the sense that they sent their goods on consignment without knowing whether or not they would sell. It was the job of the consignee to sell the consignor's merchandise at the best price obtainable. Of course, Medieval merchants did not act blindly, since they received regular reports from their correspondents about market conditions abroad. Even so, "adventuring"

[27] Malachy Postlethwayt, "Anonymous Partnerships," *The Universal Dictionary of Trade and Commerce* (2d ed.; London, 1757), I, 73. According to Postlethwayt, anonymous partnerships were temporary partnerships in which the partners traded visibly in their own names. The persons who dealt with one of the partners were presumably unaware of the existence of a partnership. After conclusion of the venture, the partners settled accounts with each other and the partnership was dissolved. Cf. Gras, *Business and Capitalism,* p. 165.

[28] For example, the Bruges branch sold almonds belonging to the firm Piero del Fede and Co. of Valencia at the Easter fair of Bergen-op-Zoom in 1441. At the same fair, the Bruges branch sold other almonds in which Piero del Fede and the Medici had a joint interest.—A.S.F., Ledger of Medici Bruges branch, fol. 232 (account of Piero del Fede and Co.).

[29] *Ibid,* fol. 250.

involved many risks because the information was never up to date and because decisions were based upon expectations which might or might not materialize. Scarcity and high prices often attracted excessive supplies and were followed by a glut on the market. If a merchant shipped goods to a place where there was a scarcity, he would frequently discover that others had been doing the same and had spoiled the market.

Although the consignment trade was predominant, there were a few exceptions to the rule. The tapestry trade was one of them. The Low Countries were the production center of tapestries which, in the fifteenth century, became the fashion. There were apparently two kinds of tapestries which differed both in kind and in quality. Those of the cheaper sort were called *verdure* ("greenery") because they were covered with foliage of a simple design. Since the same pattern was repeated over and over again, these tapestries could be cut to fit the shape of any room, like wallpaper today. They were a staple article of export and were consigned to foreign dealers in the usual way. The same was not true of the more expensive tapestries of special design which were always made to order, often according to cartoons prepared by Italian artists.[30] Usually the tapestry makers were also given the dimensions of the panels which the tapestries had to fit.[31] The Medici accepted such special orders and had them executed by the best tapestry makers in the Low Countries. Some of these tapestries were ordered by the senior partners themselves. Other orders were placed for reigning princes, cardinals, feudal lords, and other wealthy persons.[32] Probably the Medici earned only a commission on such orders.

The case of tapestries is exceptional. Most of the time the Medici had to assume risks when trading on their own account. A good example of adventuring is afforded by an account in the ledger of the Bruges branch for the year 1441. The account relates to one hundred bales of almonds which had been bought in Valencia on joint account by the firm Piero del Fede and Co. The partners in this joint venture were (1) the Medici branch in Bruges, (2) the firm Piero del Fede and Co. of Valencia, (3) Riccardo Davanzati and Co. of Barcelona and Bosco di Giovanni of Valencia. Each of the partners had a third interest in the venture. The account is very detailed and contains an itemized list of all the charges paid by the Medici branch of Bruges.[33]

30 Armand Grunzweig, *Correspondance de la filiale de Bruges des Medici* (Brussels, 1931), Part I, pp. 26, 28.

31 *Ibid.*, pp. 78 f.

32 In 1453, for example, the Medici bought tapestries for Astorre Manfredi, lord of Faenza. (They were not of the best design.)—*Ibid.*, p. 26.

33 A.S.F., Ledger of Medici Bruges Branch, fol. 246. See Appendix VIII, pp. 87–90.

These charges included first of all £55 groat paid to the captain or the scribe of the Florentine galleys for freight from Valencia to Sluys, the seaport of Bruges, and for pilotage in the harbor of Sluys. A rebate of £3 groat was granted because eleven bales had been damaged by water. In Sluys the one hundred bales were transshipped from the galleys into *schuiten* or barges and then conveyed by canal from Sluys to Bruges. The Medici paid in this connection the lighterage charges in Sluys, the customs of Damme, the freight charges from Sluys to Bruges, and the cartage charges from the quay to the warehouse in Bruges. Additional expenses were incurred on the eleven water-soaked bales, the contents of which had to be carried to an attic and spread out on the floor to dry. The Medici also paid all the expenses for freight charges, local tolls, storage, and cartage on several bales which were sent by water from Bruges to the fairs of Antwerp and Bergen-op-Zoom. The Medici further paid brokerage on sixty-nine bales sold by brokers, as well as the Catalan duties, and the Florentine consular fees in Bruges.[34] Since the bales of almonds were bought jointly with other merchants, the Medici charged the venture for storage in their own warehouses and for their commission at the rate of 1.5 per cent.

The hundred bales were sold as follows: 11 bales at the Easter fair of Bergen-op-Zoom, 20 bales at the summer fair of Antwerp, 17 bales to an Englishman named Thomas, 44 bales to local grocers in Bruges, 7 bales to a man from Brussels called Niccolò de Deril (Nicholas de Drijl), and one bale which the Medici kept for their own household. The prices obtained varied from £3 groat to £3 8*s*. groat per *carica* of 400 pounds avoirdupois, Flemish weight.[35] The gross proceeds were £313 13*s*. 5*d*. groat from which the Medici deducted £76 14*s*. 3*d*. groat for their expenses. The net proceeds of £236 19*s*. 2*d*. groat were then divided among the partners: £39 9*s*. 11*d*. groat or one sixth to Riccardo Davanzati and Co. of Barcelona, £39 9*s*. 11*d*. groat or one sixth to Bosco di Giovanni of Valencia, and two thirds or £157 19*s*. 4*d*. groat to the Medici. It seems that one of the partners, Piero del Fede and Co., withdrew from the venture and sold his share for £79 7*s*. 6*d*. groat to the Medici. The records are unfortunately incomplete. As there are no data available for the purchase cost of the almonds in Spain, it is impossible

[34] The rate of the consular fees was one sterling or one-third groat per £ groat in 1441, according to the Medici records. This rate was raised to twelve mites or one-half groat per £ gr. in 1461 and to one groat per £ gr. in 1498. Armand Grunzweig, "Le Fonds du consulat de la mer aux archives de l'Etat à Florence," *Bulletin de l'Institut Historique Belge de Rome*, X (1930), 111, 120.

[35] Franco Borlandi, ed., *El Libro di mercatantie et usanze de' paesi* (Turin, 1936), p. 126.

to determine the profit that the Medici branch of Bruges made on this venture.

It was the custom of Medieval merchants, including the Medici, to open a separate account for each venture. Such accounts were charged with all outlays, costs, and expenses, and credited with the proceeds from sales. The difference that remained after conclusion of the venture represented either a profit or a loss and was transferred to an account "Profit and Loss on Merchandise." Thus profits from trade and from exchange were kept separate. This system of opening a separate account to each venture has been called "venture accounting" by accountants and students of the history of accounting. Venture accounting eliminates the necessity of inventory valuation. Since records were generally kept according to this system, it is not surprising that Paciolo and other early authors on bookkeeping are silent on the subject of inventory valuation. Neither is it surprising that there are no examples of it in the Medici records.[36]

As the case of the one hundred bales of almonds shows, each consignment required considerable attention: shipping arrangements had to be made, warehouses hired, customs and transit charges paid, and prospective buyers approached. It was doubtless the job of the factors to attend to all these details. The role of the manager was probably to approve the bargains made by his subordinates and to see to it that the merchandise was sold as quickly as possible: the quicker the turnover, the greater were the returns on invested capital.

Venture trading rested on confidence, because the principal had little control over his agents. At best he could check whether they were cheating him by selling under the market price or by keeping part of the proceeds. Since the Medici companies dealt preferably with one another, they probably had less trouble than smaller merchants with this problem.[37]

§3. *The Alum Cartel*

The *banco* in Florence and all the Medici branches traded in commodities and dealt in exchange. In addition the Rome branch was fiscal agent of the Holy See, a function which included the transmission of papal revenues, the payment of subsidies abroad, and the exploitation

[36] Cf. Frederic C. Lane, "Venture Accounting in Medieval Business Management," *Bulletin of the Business Historical Society,* XIX (1945), 164–73.

[37] Andrea Barbarigo had considerable trouble with an agent in Syria named Dolceto, who gave him unsatisfactory service.—Frederic C. Lane, *Andrea Barbarigo, Merchant of Venice, 1418–1449* (Baltimore: The Johns Hopkins Press, 1944), p. 109.

of the Tolfa alum mines. No business records of the Rome branch being extant, it is not possible to say much on the first two topics.

As fiscal agents of the Holy See, the Medici performed the same duties as the other bankers connected with the Camera Apostolica or papal treasury. It is not true that the bankers themselves collected the proceeds from indulgences or from taxes for the papacy. For the most part such contributions were received by papal collectors, usually ecclesiastics of high rank appointed by the Pope. They turned over the receipts to the papal bankers who gave acquittance and promised to transmit the money to Rome.[38] Thus, Cristofano Spini, a factor of the Medici branch in Bruges, as proxy for Tommaso Portinari, acknowledged in a deed dated January 21, 1468 (N.S.), having received £1,773 10*s.* 3*d.* groat from Luke de Tolentis, Papal Nuncio and Archdeacon of Curzola, and promised to transmit this sum to Rome and to deliver it there to the Pope or his accredited agents.[39] This document was probably sent to Rome by the collector and enabled the Camera Apostolica to receive credit for the equivalent of £1,773 10*s.* 3*d.* groat from the Medici branch at the papal court.[40] The Medici branch in Bruges simply wrote the sum received from Luke de Tolentis to the credit of the Medici branch in Rome or to that of the *banco* in Florence. In the absence of business records, it is impossible to know how the funds were eventually transferred from Bruges to Rome; probably not by shipping specie but by exchange.

The Medici as papal bankers also received the bulls appointing new bishops. These bulls were delivered to the nominees upon payment of the annates. If the nominee delayed too long, the bull of nomination was returned to Rome. Once the Medici delivered a bull to the bishop of Nevers without having received full payment. As they had trouble collecting the unpaid balance, they threatened to write to Rome and

[38] Cf. Yves Renouard, *Les Relations des Papes d'Avignon et des compagnies commerciales et bancaires de 1316 à 1378* (Bibliothèque des Ecoles Françaises d'Athènes et de Rome, Fasc. 151, Paris, 1941), *passim;* F. Remy, *Les grandes indulgences pontificales aux Pays-Bas à la fin du moyen âge, 1300–1531* (Recueil de travaux publiés par les membres des Conférences d'Histoire et de Philologie, 2d series, XV, Louvain, 1928), *passim.*

[39] The Latin text of the acquittance and of Spini's power of attorney was published by Adolf Gottlob, "Zwei 'Instrumenta Cambii' zur Uebermittelung von Ablassgeld (1468)," *Westdeutsche Zeitschrift für Geschichte und Kunst,* XXIX (1910), 208. The English translation of the acquittance was published by William E. Lunt, *Papal Revenues in the Middle Ages* (Records of Civilization, No. XIX, New York: Columbia University Press, 1934), II, 469–74. Luke de Tolentis was in the Low Countries to raise money for the Pope's crusade against the Turks. Contributors were promised plenary indulgence after confession and penance.

[40] Georg Schneider, "Die finanziellen Beziehungen der florentinischen Bankiers zur Kirche von 1285 bis 1304," *Schmoller's staats- und socialwissenschaftliche Forschungen,* XVII (1900), 34; cf. Lunt, *Papal Revenues,* I, 52–54.

to have the bishop excommunicated.[41] In another case, the Medici wrote to John Kemp, Cardinal and Archbishop of York, that they had secured the appointment of his nephew Thomas Kemp to the bishopric of London in preference to a rival candidate supported by Henry VI and William de la Pole, first Duke of Suffolk.[42] The Medici probably had some reason to court the favor of John Kemp, but who would expect the appointment of bishops to fall within the range of a merchant's activities? [43]

The papacy not only collected revenue abroad but also paid subsidies to foreign princes who had trouble with the Turks or with heretics such as the Hussites of Bohemia. Papal subsidies to Matthias Corvinus, King of Hungary (1458–1490), whose dominions were threatened by the Turks, were paid in bills of exchange on the Medici branch in Venice.[44] There was no organized money market in as backward a country as Hungary. The bills were presumably paid either to the king's agents or to Venetian merchants who traded in Hungary.

The Medici probably allowed the Camera Apostolica to overdraw its account in anticipation of revenues. According to a settlement made in 1473, the Medici were creditors of the Camera Apostolica to the extent of Fl. 62,918 *di camera.*[45]

Through their connections at the papal court, the Medici were able in 1466 to acquire an interest in the Societas Aluminum, a company which farmed the Tolfa alum mines. From then on the Medici strove to control the alum market in western Europe and to establish a monopoly. In the Middle Ages, alum was an essential product because of its general use as a mordant in the dyeing of textiles. Until the mid-fifteenth century, high-quality alum was produced mainly in the Levant, and the Turks, in whose territory the mines were located, exacted excessive royalties. There were other alum deposits both in Europe and in North Africa, but their output was either poor in quality or insufficient to meet the demand. Alum from the Barbary Coast reached Bruges in limited quantities. In Christendom, only the mines of Volterra, in Florentine territory, and of Ischia, a small island off the Italian coast near

41 Grunzweig, *Correspondance*, pp. xxiii, 1–4, 13–15.

42 The firm Piero de' Medici and Co. in Bruges to the Cardinal of York, December 5, 1448 (*ibid.*, pp. 13–15). Cf. T. F. Tout, "John Kemp," *Dictionary of National Biography*, XXX, 387.

43 The Medici agents also concerned themselves with the hiring of tenors and the recruiting of choir boys for the Sistine Chapel and even participated in the hunt for lost classics. Grunzweig, *Correspondance*, p. xxiii; Sieveking, *Handlungsbücher der Medici*, p. 28.

44 Gottlob, "Zwei 'Instrumenta Cambii' zur Uebermittelung," *Westdeutsche Zeitschrift*, XXIX, 205.

45 Lunt, *Papal Revenues*, I, 322–23.

Naples, produced a somewhat better grade of alum. This was the situation when, in 1459, rich deposits of high-quality alum were discovered by one Giovanni de Castro at Tolfa near Civitavecchia in the Papal States.[46]

According to the agreement of 1466, the Societas Aluminum, in which the Medici had become partners, took over the exploitation of the Tolfa mines and the sale of the entire output but agreed to pay a royalty of two ducats to the Camera Apostolica for each *cantaro* of alum taken from the papal warehouses in Civitavecchia.[47] All the alum mined at Tolfa was to be stored in those warehouses in order to prevent any leakage to the detriment of the papal treasury. Nothing could be taken from the warehouses except in the presence of a papal official. In addition to the royalty, the Camera Apostolica was to receive two thirds of all extra profits.

The mining of alum near Volterra was apparently discouraged after the Medici acquired an interest in the Tolfa mines. As the citizens of Volterra were thus deprived of a source of income, they revolted against Florentine rule. Lorenzo was evidently interested in keeping the mines under Florentine, that is, under Medici control. He did not hesitate to use all his political influence with the Signoria and to recommend energetic measures to suppress the revolt. An army was sent to subdue Volterra which surrendered after a siege. The unfortunate town was most cruelly sacked by the victors, and the alum mines remained under Florentine control.

The next step was to get rid of the competition of Turkish alum. The Pope did not hesitate to use his spiritual powers to attain this aim. The income which the Camera Apostolica derived from the Tolfa mines was earmarked for the crusade against the Turks and the Hussite heretics of Bohemia. As a logical consequence, to trade in Turkish alum was unquestionably to give aid to the infidel and deprive the crusade of financial support. The Pope, therefore, forbade the importation of Turkish alum in all Christian lands. Those who disregarded this prohibition were liable to ecclesiastical censures. Cargoes of Turkish alum were declared contrabrand and were seizable by anyone either in port

[46] G. Zippel, "L'Allume di Tolfa e il suo commercio," *Archivio della R. Società Romana di Storia Patria,* XXX (1907), 5–51, 389–461; Jakob Strieder, *Studien zur Geschichte kapitalistischer Organisationsformen* (Munich, 1925), pp. 168–83; Roman Piotrowski, *Cartels and Trusts: Their Origin and Historical Development from the Economic and Legal Aspects* (London: G. Allen and Unwin, 1933), pp. 153–59.

[47] Strieder, *Studien,* p. 170. Zippel, "L'Allume di Tolfa," *Archivio della Società Romana,* XXX, 405, analyzes in detail the contract of 1466. The royalty was later reduced to one ducat per *cantaro.* The *cantaro* was a unit of weight of about 150 lbs. avoirdupois.

or on the high seas, but the lessees of the Tolfa mines and the papal treasury claimed a share of the prizes.

The only remaining competition was that of the Ischia mines in the kingdom of Naples. In order to do away with this competitor, too, the Rome branch of the Medici in 1470 entered into a twenty-five-year cartel agreement with the farmer of the Ischia mines. The deal received the approval of the Pope and of the King of Naples as owners of the Tolfa and Ischia mines respectively. The purpose of the agreement was avowedly to suppress ruinous competition, "because the oversupply of alum had depressed prices." [48] In reality, the parties to the contract intended to establish a monopoly, to restrict output, to keep up prices, and to regulate the sale of alum according to a quota system.

The agreement stipulated that the exploitation of the mines should remain in the hands of the lessees but it forbade them to sell independently without each other's knowledge. The proceeds of all sales were to be divided equally between the two members of the cartel, unless one of them was unable to supply his full quota. In such a case profits were to be shared proportionately to the quota actually supplied by each member.

The two contracting parties agreed to sell only at the price fixed by the cartel. If one of them sold below that price he had to make good the loss incurred by the other party.

The cartel agreement became effective immediately, but certain exceptions were made with respect to the stores of alum which the lessees of the papal mines had accumulated in Flanders and in Venice. The agreement did not apply to these two markets until the existing stocks had been sold. In the meantime the other party was to receive one sixth of the profits as compensation.

Any violation of the cartel agreement entailed a penalty of fifty thousand ducats. The payment of this enormous fine did not relieve the offender from his obligation to comply with the terms of the cartel agreement.

The contract of 1470 was much more than an attempt to "corner" the market. The long duration of the contract and its detailed provisions make it a full-fledged cartel agreement, although some economists will maintain, against all evidence, that cartels are a modern phenomenon and did not exist prior to 1873.[49] Those are, of course, the same people who believe that business cycles are a product of the Industrial

[48] Strieder, *Studien,* p. 176; Piotrowski, *Cartels,* pp. 155 f.
[49] Piotrowski, *Cartels,* pp. 11–86.

Revolution and that, prior to that time, there was no alternation of good and bad times of a "recurrent" or "cyclical" character.[50]

It is difficult to deny that the formation of the alum cartel was inconsistent with the teachings of the church.[51] The canonist writers were outspoken in their condemnation of monopoly. They knew very well that a monopolist restricts output and raises his price "for his own private gain and benefit" and "in prejudice of the public."[52] The papacy was not unaware of the discrepancy between its policy in the matter of the alum cartel and the doctrines professed by the church in the matter of social ethics. The Curia condoned its policy with regard to the alum cartel on the questionable principle that the end justifies the means.[53]

The cartel was only a partial success because of the opposition of vested interests and the ineffectiveness of the ban on Turkish alum. True, the price of alum increased considerably, but this very increase encouraged interloping. The Pope resorted to diplomacy in order to stop the evasion of his decrees. He tried in vain to secure legislation against the introduction of Turkish alum in England, Flanders, and Venice.[54] In England the Pope's emissaries made no headway, probably because Edward IV, whose throne was by no means secure, could not afford to antagonize the English merchants and the clothiers who were violently opposed to the alum monopoly.

In Venice the Curia succeeded in 1469 in concluding an agreement with Bartolomeo Giorgio, the main dealer in alum, by giving him the

[50] James Arthur Estey, *Business Cycles; Their Nature, Cause, and Control* (New York: Prentice-Hall, 1941), pp. 45–47, gives a characteristic formulation of this theory: business cycles do not antedate the Napoleonic Wars; prior to that time business fluctuations did not follow "a recognizable pattern" and were not caused by factors "inherent" in the economic system. Joseph A. Schumpeter is a notable exception among the theorists of business cycles. He stresses the importance of "external" factors and admits that business cycles have a long history.—*Business Cycles; A Theoretical, Historical, and Statistical Analysis of the Capitalist Process* (New York: McGraw-Hill Book Company, 1939), I, pp. 220 ff. The merchant manuals of the Middle Ages refer repeatedly and emphatically to seasonal variations in the money market which followed a definite and well-known pattern. Are seasonal variations not of a recurrent, cyclical, or rhythmic character? If they are seasonal, they must necessarily be recurrent.

[51] A. Fanfani, *Le Origini dello spirito capitalistico in Italia* (Milan, 1933), pp. 109, 110, 123, quotes San Antonino, Archbishop of Florence, San Bernardino of Siena, and Tommaso de Vio, better known as Cardinal Cajetan, who all condemn monopoly as a violation of commutative justice and of the just price. Cf. Strieder, *Studien*, p. 162; Piotrowski, *Cartels*, pp. 154 f.

[52] Cf. George O'Brien, *An Essay on Medieval Economic Teaching* (London: Longmans, Green and Company, 1920), p. 124.

[53] The canonists considered a monopoly privileged by the state as lawful. Moreover, they did not question the right of the state to levy tolls and to put indirect taxes on commodities. The papacy could justify its action on these grounds.

[54] Zippel, "L'Allume di Tolfa," *Archivio della Società Romana*, XXX, 47–49, 389–98; Strieder, *Studien*, pp. 178–80.

exclusive right of selling papal alum in Venetian territory, Lombardy, Romagna, southern Germany, and Austria. In return for this concession, he pledged himself to exclude Turkish alum from the Venetian market and to take 6,000 *cantari* a year of the rival, papal product.[55] The conclusion of this agreement was undoubtedly facilitated by the fact that Venice was at war with the Turks from 1463 to 1479.

In Flanders the papal envoys could count on the support of Tommaso Portinari who was of the Duke's council. As long as Philip the Good was alive the negotiations made little progress, but Portinari was a favorite of Charles the Bold, Philip's son and successor. After he came to power, in 1467, the negotiations progressed more satisfactorily. A treaty was signed on May 4, 1468, by which the Duke prohibited the importation of Turkish alum and was to receive 6*s*. groat for each *cantaro* of papal alum imported into the Low Countries. A clause of the treaty provided that the cartel could not charge more than the price at which alum of whatever origin was sold in neighboring states. Despite this clause, which protected the consumer against unfair competition, the treaty had to be shelved because it aroused so much opposition on the part of the representatives of the towns in the Estates General. A new plenipotentiary, Tommaso di Vincenti da Fana, was sent by the Pope to the Low Countries to demand the fulfillment of the agreement and the exclusion of Turkish alum. His mission was a failure. The opposition to the cartel did not subside; it continued unabated all through the reign of Charles the Bold.[56]

There are indications that alum from Asia Minor and from the Barbary Coast continued to be imported into the Low Countries in competition with papal alum. One of the principal importers was apparently the Florentine banking house of the Pazzi, the great rivals of the Medici in business as well as in politics.[57]

Persistent competition and opposition from organized consumer groups were not the only difficulties encountered by the cartel. There were administrative problems, too. Lack of co-ordination was one source of trouble. The Bruges branch of the Medici apparently sold the alum on commission for the Rome branch. The two branches came into conflict as early as 1464, even before the formation of the cartel.

[55] The same Bartolomeo Giorgio had been the farmer of the alum mines in Asia Minor up to 1463, when he had to leave Turkey because of the war. W. Heyd, *Histoire du commerce du Levant* (Leipzig, 1923), II, 328.

[56] Grunzweig, *Correspondance*, pp. xxi f.

[57] L. Gilliodts-van Severen, *Cartulaire de l'Estaple* (Bruges, 1905), II, 164, No. 1108; 229, No. 1189.

Already at that time the Medici were trying to control the market for alum. Roberto Martelli, the manager of the Rome branch, was apparently so dissatisfied with the Medici company in Bruges that he sent as a special agent to Flanders a Sienese by the name of Niccolò Spanocchi.

Martelli's impatience, according to Portinari, was not justified. In his opinion the papal mines produced excessive quantities of alum so that it was almost impossible to maintain prices. No more alum should be shipped to Bruges until the existing stocks were sold. The Pope, Portinari thought, should follow the example of the Genoese who, when they controlled the alum mines of Asia Minor, had known how to adjust supply to demand. Portinari further complained that Spanocchi had so little experience that, if he had been in charge of the sale of alum, prices would have fallen to one third of those obtained by the Bruges branch. Portinari stressed that able management (*buon governo*) was required in order to prevent competitors from breaking in, and that prices would never recover if they were allowed to sag.[58]

It appears from later letters that Spanocchi's presence in Bruges did more harm than good. Angelo Tani and Tommaso Portinari were glad that new shipments of alum were not consigned to Spanocchi, as Roberto Martelli had announced; otherwise it would have been difficult to maintain prices.[59] The newly arrived alum was expected to sell quickly provided none came to Bruges from other sources.[60] The Bruges branch hoped that Cosimo would give them a share in the alum business instead of only a commission.[61] In another letter, Spanocchi's recall was requested, and Portinari again stressed that the dissatisfaction of the Rome branch was without foundation.[62]

The alum cartel was dissolved in 1478 when Sixtus IV confiscated all Medici property in the Papal States, after the failure of the Pazzi conspiracy.[63] The Medici never regained control of the alum market, although part of their claims on the Camera Apostolica were later paid by assignment on the output of the Tolfa mines.[64]

58 Tommaso Portinari to Cosimo de' Medici, February 15, 1464 (N.S.).—Grunzweig, *Correspondance*, pp. 106 f.

59 Tommaso Portinari and Angelo Tani to Cosimo de' Medici, March 28, 1464.—*Ibid.*, p. 112.

60 One should not forget that the war between Venice and the Turks probably prevented the arrival of the Turkish alum.

61 Tommaso Portinari and Angelo Tani to Cosimo de' Medici, April 29, 1464.—*Ibid.*, pp. 118 f.

62 Tommaso Portinari to Cosimo de' Medici, May 14, 1464.—*Ibid.*, p. 132. The letters after 1464 contain more about the alum business.—*Ibid.*, p. xxii. Their publication as Volume II of the *Correspondance* has been delayed by the war.

63 Strieder, *Studien*, p. 180. The Medici were replaced by the Genoese firm Domenico Centurioni and Giovanni Doria and Co.

64 Zippel, "L'Allume di Tolfa," *Archivio della Società Romana*, XXX, 415.

The alum cartel was an early manifestation of a new development. Prior to the fifteenth century, the sedentary merchants did not have enough capital to establish permanent monopolies. It is true that corners were fairly common, but they did not outlast the first change in market conditions. The appearance of powerful banking houses with a network of branches and correspondents made it possible for one firm to gain monopoly control or for several firms to form combinations "in restraint of trade." This new trend gained momentum during the sixteenth century with the mining cartels sponsored by the Fuggers and reached a climax in the seventeenth century with the development of joint-stock companies and the monopolistic organization of colonial trade.[65]

§4. *The Sources of Invested Funds*

The power of the Medici as a banking house, and their weakness also, become clearer when we examine the source of their funds. The main problem is whether the Medici bank operated mainly with the money invested by the partners or whether most of the operating capital was supplied from outside sources. It would be easy to settle this question if some balance sheets of the Medici bank were still available. As none have come down to us, another method of approach has to be used.

According to the partnership agreement of 1471, the Medici company in Bruges had a capital of only £3,000 groat. And yet the Bruges branch was able to lend £6,000 groat, and more, to the Duke of Burgundy. Besides, there was money to spare which was invested in mercantile ventures and in the business of exchange. The obvious conclusion is that the Medici branch of Bruges operated with financial resources which were much larger than its capital. The same holds true of the *banco* in Florence and of the other branches.

From where did these extra funds come? A careful examination of the surviving records reveals that the Medici bank in Florence and its subsidiaries abroad were financed largely as follows: (1) by undistributed profits that were allowed to accumulate; (2) by money invested by the partners themselves *fuori del corpo della compagnia,* that is, above and beyond the capital; and (3) by money held on deposit or *a discrezione* for outsiders.

As has been pointed out, the articles of association usually provided that profits could not be withdrawn before the termination of the

[65] Gras, *Business and Capitalism,* p. 123, remarks that this development should be made the object of further study.

contract. The private account book of Francesco Sassetti proves conclusively that this practice was actually followed and that profits were divided only from time to time.[66] Moreover, substantial reserves were set aside and kept undivided in order to provide for unforeseen contingencies. Sassetti's account book contains data concerning only the Geneva and Lyons branches, but there is no reason to suppose that a different practice was followed elsewhere.

According to the articles of association, each partner was bound to supply in full his share of the capital, but he was free to invest additional money *fuori del corpo* or outside the capital. On such investments he was entitled to receive interest which was payable prior to any division of profits among the partners. Thus Sassetti had, in 1462, more than 6,000 *écus* on deposit with the Geneva branch in addition to a share of 2,300 *écus* in the capital. The Medici themselves placed money on deposit with the *banco* in Florence and with the branches outside of Florence. Cosimo de' Medici and his brother Lorenzo had Fl. 10,000 on deposit with the *banco* in Florence and another Fl. 10,000 with the Medici company in Venice, according to the Florentine tax records for the year 1430.[67] On these deposits, the two brothers received 5 per cent. It even happened that one branch had money on deposit with another branch and received a given per cent for the use of this money. Thus the Medici partnership in Venice was, in 1459, a creditor of the Medici partnership in Milan for a deposit of £15,000 *imperiali* on which the latter paid interest at the rate of 12 per cent. The interest was only 10 per cent on another deposit of 2,000 ducats or £7,800 *imperiali*.[68]

The Medici bank and its subsidiaries also accepted deposits from outsiders. These deposits were not demand deposits, but time deposits on which interest or *discrezione* was paid. This word *discrezione* was used with three different meanings in the Florentine records of the time. First, it meant that a deposit was an irregular deposit, that is, that the borrower had the right to employ the funds in his business "at his discretion" or as he saw fit. Second, *discrezione* referred to the return which was paid on such deposits by the borrower. Third, the word *discrezione* was used to designate the deposit itself.[69]

[66] Florence Edler de Roover, "Francesco Sassetti and the Downfall of the Medici Banking House," *Bulletin of the Business Historical Society*, XVII (1943), 72–75.

[67] Heinrich Sieveking, *Aus Genueser Rechnungs- und Steuerbüchern* (Sitzungsberichte der Kais. Akademie der Wissenschaften in Wien, Philosophisch-historische Klasse, No. CLXII. Vienna, 1909), p. 97.

[68] Sieveking, *Handlungsbücher der Medici*, p. 37 .

[69] F. E. de Roover, "Francesco Sassetti," *Bulletin of the Business Historical Society*, XVII, 71.

The outsiders who had deposit accounts with the Medici bank were mainly prominent Florentines friendly to the Medici, and Italian nobles, ecclesiastics, and statesmen who, for some reason or other, did not want to invest all their fortunes in landed estates, in annuities, in *rentes* (a form of mortgage), or even in municipal loans. These investors were certainly attracted by the high return which was promised to depositors by the Medici and other merchant bankers. Francesco Sassetti, the general manager of the Medici, had most of his fortune, 68.6 per cent in 1462 and 70.9 per cent in 1466, invested in trade and banking. His shares in the capital of the Avignon and Geneva branches were only a small portion of his business investments. The major part—49.1 per cent out of 68.6 per cent in 1462—was made up of deposits with the Medici bank.[70] Although Sassetti had no share in the capital of the Medici branch in Milan, he had Fl. 5,000 *larghi* standing to his credit on the books of that branch. According to the entries in his private account book, the Medici company of Milan held this money "on deposit and at their discretion" and paid interest on it at the rate of 10 per cent a year. Notice of withdrawal had to be given a year in advance.[71] In other cases this time was reduced to six or three months.[72]

Foreigners also had money on deposit with the Medici bank. The Lyons branch, for example, had among its depositors two prominent Frenchmen: Ymbert de Batarnay, Seigneur du Bouchage, chamberlain of the King of France, and Messire Philippe de Commines, a diplomat of Flemish origin and the author of famous memoirs of the reign of Louis XI. The Medici branch in Bruges was used as a depository for idle funds by the Count of Campo Basso, Charles the Bold's Italian *condottiere,* and by Guillaume Bische, another prominent figure at the Burgundian court. Bische played a double game and eventually betrayed his master by going over to the French.[73]

It was not without cause that politicians, such as Commines or Bische, were eager to place some of their funds with international bankers. They wanted some investment that was safe from confisca-

[70] *Ibid.*, pp. 69 f. See Appendixes I, II, III, pp. 67–72.

[71] "Piero et Johanni de' Medici e Compagnia di Milano deono dare F. cinquemila larghi di Firenze . . . . et tengonli in diposito a loro discretione, posti a Valsente a c. 2—F. 5,000 larghi, F. 6,000 di suggello E. deono dare F. cinquecento larghi per discretione de' detti danari insino a tutto l'anno 1463 d'accordo con loro posti in questo a c. 20—F. 500 larghi, F. 600 di suggello."—Florence, Archivio di Stato, Carte Strozziane, Series II, No. 20: Libro segreto di Francesco Sassetti, 1462–1472, fol. 11. See pp. 71–72.

[72] *Ibid.*, fol. 21.

[73] Grunzweig, *Correspondance,* pp. xxiii, xxxvi.

tion should they fall into disgrace or have to flee the country. Real estate could not be concealed, but accounts with an international banking house could be whisked out of the country with a stroke of the pen. A book transfer of two lines was all that was necessary. The contract between Ymbert de Batarnay and the Medici company in Lyons provided that the money received on deposit by the latter was repayable at the depositor's option either in Lyons or in any of the other places where the Medici had branches.[74] Philippe de Commines drew on his deposit account with the Lyons branch to bribe his way out of the iron cage in which he was locked up for plotting against Anne de Beaujeu, regent of France during the minority of Charles VIII.[75] Guillaume Bische was not so lucky as Commines. After Bische had betrayed Maximilian of Austria, in 1480, Tommaso Portinari was called to the court at Brussels. He was forced to take an oath on the Gospels and to reveal how much Bische had standing to his credit in his deposit account. Maximilian of Austria confiscated the balance. Bische, however, recovered his funds more than fourteen years later, also by resorting to coercive and illegal methods. He took advantage of Charles VIII's campaign in Italy to extort an indemnity of Fl. 17,500 from the Florentine republic (1494–1495).[76]

The taking of interest, as has been pointed out, was considered usury by the church. How was the payment of interest on bank deposits reconcilable with the prohibition of usury? The answer to this question raises many subtle problems and will therefore be only tentative.

The entries in Sassetti's private account book show conclusively that he received a fixed return on his deposits and that the rate varied from 8 to 12 per cent a year on different deposits.[77] However, the contract between the Medici company in Lyons and Ymbert de Batarnay, Seigneur du Bouchage, concerning a deposit of 10,000 *écus au soleil* does not mention any fixed percentage but states, on the contrary, that this sum was to be employed in lawful trade and the profits accruing therefrom were to be shared equally between the contracting parties.[78] This clause should not be interpreted too literally, since it is unlikely that the Medici shared their profits with depositors. It meant,

[74] Giuseppe Molini, *Documenti di storia italiana* (Florence, 1836–37), I, 14.

[75] Baron Kervyn de Lettenhove, *Lettres et négotiations de Philippe de Commines* (Brussels, 1867), II, 39, 68.

[76] Grunzweig, *Correspondance*, p. xxxvi.

[77] Sometimes the rate is explicitly stated and sometimes not. "E deono dare ∇ 480 vecchi per providigione d'uno anno di ∇ 6,000 a 8 per cento l'anno."—Florence, Archivio di Stato, Carte Strozziane, Series II, No. 20, fol. 12, Account of Francesco Sassetti e Compagnia di Ginevra.

[78] Molini, *Documenti*, I, 14.

however, that the depositor received a return which might vary slightly from year to year, sometimes more, if the year had been good, and sometimes less, if it had been poor.[79] If there were losses instead of profits, the depositor might not receive any return at all. According to a statement of account attached to the contract, the Seigneur du Bouchage was allowed 1,535 *écus sans soleil* for an unstated period ending February 12, 1491, and 1,640 *écus sans soleil* for the two succeeding years ending in May 1493.[80] The rate of return was probably 7.5 per cent in the first case and 8 per cent in the second, but this is more or less a guess.[81] In any case, it seems that deposits with the Medici bank could be compared to modern income bonds on which interest is paid only when earned. The correctness of this interpretation seems to be confirmed by the story of Philippe de Commines' troubles with the Medici bank.

Commines, too, had money on deposit with the Lyons branch. A settlement of account took place in November 1489, and the parties agreed on everything except one point: the Medici company in Lyons refused to allow anything to Commines as return on his deposit for the last two years. The parties agreed, however, to submit the difference to Lorenzo the Magnificent.[82] It must be added that the Lyons branch was at this time in serious financial difficulties and had suffered heavy losses because of the mismanagement of Lionetto de' Rossi, the operating partner. Commines felt that he had not received a square deal and wrote to his dear friend "Seigneur Laurent" (Lorenzo the Magnificent). Seigneur Laurent replied that he was very sorry, of course, but that he had lost a great deal and that there was little which he could do.[83] Commines accepted Lorenzo's decision, but not without complaining that such a settlement was very unfavorable to him.[84] He was given to believe that if the Medici bank recouped its losses as it hoped, all would be made good.[85] But Lorenzo died in 1492, his son Piero was expelled from Florence in 1494, and all Medici property was confiscated by the new republican regime. Commines tried

79 Florence Edler [de Roover] gives a good example of a reduction of the rate of return paid to depositors when operating results were unfavorable, in "Eclaircissements à propos des considérations de R. Davidsohn sur la productivité de l'argent au moyen âge," *Vierteljahrschrift für Sozial- und Wirtschaftsgeschichte,* XXX (1937), 377–78.

80 Molini, *Documenti,* I, 16.

81 It is impossible to compute the rate with accuracy because the *écu sans soleil* was worth a little less than the *écu au soleil.*

82 Kervyn de Lettenhove, *Lettres,* II, 69 f.

83 *Ibid.,* pp. 70 f.

84 "Le dit appointement est bien mègre pour moi."—*Ibid.,* p. 72.

85 *Ibid,* p. 83.

to obtain payment from the Florentine republic and wrote one request after another for the next fifteen years.[86] It was all in vain; he never received either principal or interest.

Why were the Medici so firm in refusing to credit Philippe de Commines for interest on his deposit? The explanation, in my opinion, is found in the provisions of a Florentine statute of the year 1312. Because usury was prohibited, interest was not recoverable at law. The statute in question provided, however, that any interest or "consideration" was due to the creditor if it had been written to his credit in the books of the debtor. Such credits were not to be considered as usury, since the debtor had made the entry in his books of his own free will and without compulsion.[87] Therefore, if interest had been added to the credit of Commines, he would automatically have become a creditor of the Medici bank to that extent. As long as no interest was credited to his account, he had no legal claim to any return. The statute of 1312 also throws light on a puzzling passage in a letter of Tommaso Portinari: "Our profits, as you will see [from the balance sheet], have been small this year and our expenses, great. I have not added any *discrezione* to several deposit accounts."[88]

The effect of the usury prohibition was to place the creditor at the mercy of the debtor, since it made it difficult for the former to collect interest from the latter. Another result was that merchants resorted to all kinds of subterfuges in order to conceal interest charges. Documents were deliberately couched in obscure and ambiguous language that became a fertile breeding ground for expensive litigation. It was not even clear whether persons who had given money in deposit to a banker should be considered as creditors or as partners. In 1487, the heirs of Tommaso Soderini, a prominent Florentine and supporter of the Medici, brought suit against Tommaso Portinari, who had by that time broken his connection with the Medici and was doing business on his own account, for restitution of a sum of 4,204½ ducats which he had received in deposit and which was repayable after four months'

[86] *Ibid.*, pp. 147, 248–49, 255–56, 269–73. The last request is dated August 25, 1511. Commines died the same year.

[87] Armand Grunzweig, "Le Fonds de la Mercanzia aux Archives d'Etat de Florence au point de vue de l'histoire de Belgique," *Bulletin de l'Institut Historique Belge de Rome,* XI (1932), 92 f; Gustav Lastig, "Beiträge zur Geschichte des Handelsrechts," *Zeitschrift für das gesamte Handelsrecht,* XXIII (1878), 143–47. This passage of the Florentine statute of 1312 has apparently not attracted the attention of the authors who have discussed the legal character of the deposit or *accomandigia* contract. Cf. Armando Sapori, "Le compagnie mercantili toscane del Dugento e dei primi del Trecento: la responsabilità dei compagni verso i terzi," reprinted from *Studi di storia e diritto in onore di Enrico Besta* (Milan, 1938), pp. 8–15.

[88] Grunzweig, *Correspondance,* p. 131.

advance notice. Portinari refused to return the amount and contended that it had not been given to him in deposit, but that there existed a partnership because it had been agreed between the parties to employ the money in trade and to share the profits accruing therefrom.[89] The real reason for Portinari's refusal was that he was hard up for cash and desperately short of working capital. The court ordered Portinari to give bail for the sum in dispute but did not decide immediately on the main issue of the suit. Unfortunately, we do not know how the court finally settled the case.

To receive interest on a bank deposit was severely condemned as usury by San Antonino, Archbishop of Florence. In his works he inveighs against nobles who do not work but set out their money with a trader or a banker in expectation of a return "at the discretion" of the latter and without assuming any risks.[90] These views were even shared by merchants. Lodovico Guicciardini, a Florentine residing in Antwerp in the sixteenth century, severely criticizes gentlemen who, for the sake of a "certain" gain, place their money on deposit with merchants instead of improving their estates.[91]

It may be argued that the prohibition of usury impeded the development of capitalism in at least two ways: first, by keeping the interest rate high and, second, by undermining the enforcement of contracts. As far as the Medici are concerned, unsound financing was perhaps a major factor in their downfall. It seems plausible that they placed themselves in the same position as that of a modern corporation which is trading on the equity and relies mostly on the issuing of bonds as a means of financing expansion. When business conditions became unfavorable and profits fell, the Medici should have reduced the return which they offered to depositors. Perhaps it was impossible to do so without losing prestige or without causing withdrawals of much needed cash at a critical moment. In any case the Medici were reluctant to cut interest charges, except as a last resort. When they finally decided to take this fateful step, it gave wide publicity to the extent of their losses and undermined their prestige both at home and abroad.[92] Lorenzo the Magnificent was able to maintain himself in

89 *The heirs of Tommaso Soderini* v. *Tommaso Portinari,* September 11, 1487; Gilliodts, *Cartulaire de l'Estaple,* II, 260, No. 1240.

90 Bede Jarrett, O.P., *San Antonino and Medieval Economics* (St. Louis, 1914), p. 69; Fanfani, *Spirito capitalistico,* p. 113.

91 R. H. Tawney and Eileen Power, eds., *Tudor Economic Documents,* III, 161.

92 Alfred von Reumont, *Lorenzo de' Medici, the Magnificent* (London, 1876), II, 334–37. On one day, April 21, 1488, seventeen letters about the difficulties of the Lyons branch were dispatched to foreign creditors, including Ymbert de Batarnay, Seigneur du Bouchage.

power, but Piero, his son, was overthrown in 1494, a little more than two years after his father's death.

§5. *The Causes of the Decline*

Machiavelli, in his *History of Florence,* blames the downfall of the Medici banking house on Lorenzo's lack of business ability and on the extravagant conduct of the branch managers who behaved like princes rather than private individuals.[93] Adam Smith, who was well read, made the most of this passage of Machiavelli's to prove the wastefulness and inefficiency of government enterprises.[94] There is undoubtedly much truth in Machiavelli's statement; Lorenzo was certainly a poor businessman.[95] But Adam Smith oversimplifies the problem. Mrs. de Roover has pointed out in her study of Francesco Sassetti that "the downfall of the Medici banking house cannot be traced to a single cause, but to a complex of circumstances and a combination of interacting factors." [96] Francesco Sassetti was at least partly responsible because of his failure to keep the branch managers firmly in hand. Besides the faults of Lorenzo and Francesco Sassetti, there are other factors that should be considered.

Business conditions were in general unfavorable after 1465, and the value of the gold florin in silver *piccioli* rose more than 20 per cent between 1475 and 1495 (see chart on page 61). This rise was not due solely to the debasement of the silver currency, but also to a change in the market ratio between gold and silver. Since most deposits were repayable in gold, the Medici were crushed between the steady fall of gold prices and the mounting burden of their commitments to depositors.

In Florence small payments were made in silver or *lire di piccioli.* For example, all retail prices and wage rates were quoted in *piccioli.* But, according to law, all wholesale prices were quoted in gold florins and all bills of exchange were payable in the same currency. In other words the *lira di piccioli* or the pound of 240 *denari piccioli* was used in the making of local payments, but the gold florin was used

93 Niccolò Machiavelli, *Istorie fiorentine,* ed. Plinio Carli (Florence, 1927), Vol. II, Book VIII, chap. xxxvi, p. 218.

94 Adam Smith, *An Inquiry into the Nature and Causes of the Wealth of Nations* (New York: Modern Library, 1937), p. 771.

95 There are other testimonies beside Machiavelli's. For example, Alessandro de' Pazzi, a nephew of Lorenzo, states that the latter "did not have much aptitude for trade" ("non era alla mercatura molto atto").—"Discorso di Alessandro de' Pazzi al cardinale Giulio de' Medici, anno 1522," *Archivio storico italiano,* Series 1, Vol. I (1842), p. 422.

96 F. E. de Roover, "Francesco Sassetti," *Bulletin of the Business Historical Society,* XVII, 80.

exclusively in banking and in international trade. Retailers kept their books in *piccioli,* but merchants and bankers kept theirs in gold florins. Industrial entrepreneurs used both monetary units in their books. Accounts in the general ledger were in florins but records concerning wages and supplies were kept in *lire di piccioli,* the silver currency. After 1450, the local price level was presumably stabilized by debasing the silver coinage. But wholesale commodity prices (usually quoted in florins) were allowed to fall, because the public authorities were reluctant to reduce the gold contents of the florin and to destroy its prestige as an international currency.

The Medici lost in more than one way: first because gold prices of commodities fell steadily, and secondly because much business was done with countries, such as France, England, and Flanders, whose silver currency was depreciating in terms of gold. What the Medici might have gained on wages and other small items was probably negligible. While assets thus tended to shrink in value, liabilities remained the same because the Medici owed gold—florins or *écus*—to depositors. As the purchasing power of gold increased, interest charges payable in gold became more and more burdensome. But the worst was that the assets, as they declined in value, reduced the owner's equity, until there was nothing left. The Medici, by relying so much on borrowed capital, had weakened their resistance to deflationary pressures and were especially vulnerable when the crisis came.

As was pointed out before, the Medici feared the adverse effect on their credit of a reduction of the "discretion" which they offered to depositors. The evil of delaying such a reduction was aggravated by the defects of the financial structure: a small capital and a large debt on which interest had to be paid. As long as earnings exceeded interest charges, profits were likely to be great. If, however, earnings failed to cover those charges, losses too were likely to be large and to swallow up the capital within a short time.

During Cosimo's earlier years, the Medici business had grown through the reinvestment of earnings. But, as the family rose to princely status, household expenses grew to such an extent that earnings were taken out instead of being plowed back.[97] Those with-

[97] Alessandro de' Pazzi lists as causes of the failure of the Medici bank: (1) Lorenzo's lack of business ability, (2) his interest in politics, (3) his high household expenses.—"Discorso," *Archivio storico italiano,* Series I, Vol. I (1842), 422. According to Lorenzo's own statement, from 1434 to 1471, or in the space of thirty-eight years, his family spent the incredible sum of Fl. 663,755 or an average of Fl. 17,467 a year on buildings, charities, subsidies, and taxes, not including other expenses.—William Roscoe, *The Life of Lorenzo de' Medici* (9th ed.; London, 1847), p. 426; Angelo Fabroni, *Laurentii Medicis Magnifici Vita* (Pisa, 1784), II, 47.

RATE OF THE GOLD FLORIN IN LIRE AND SOLDI PICCIOLI

FROM 1415 TO 1515

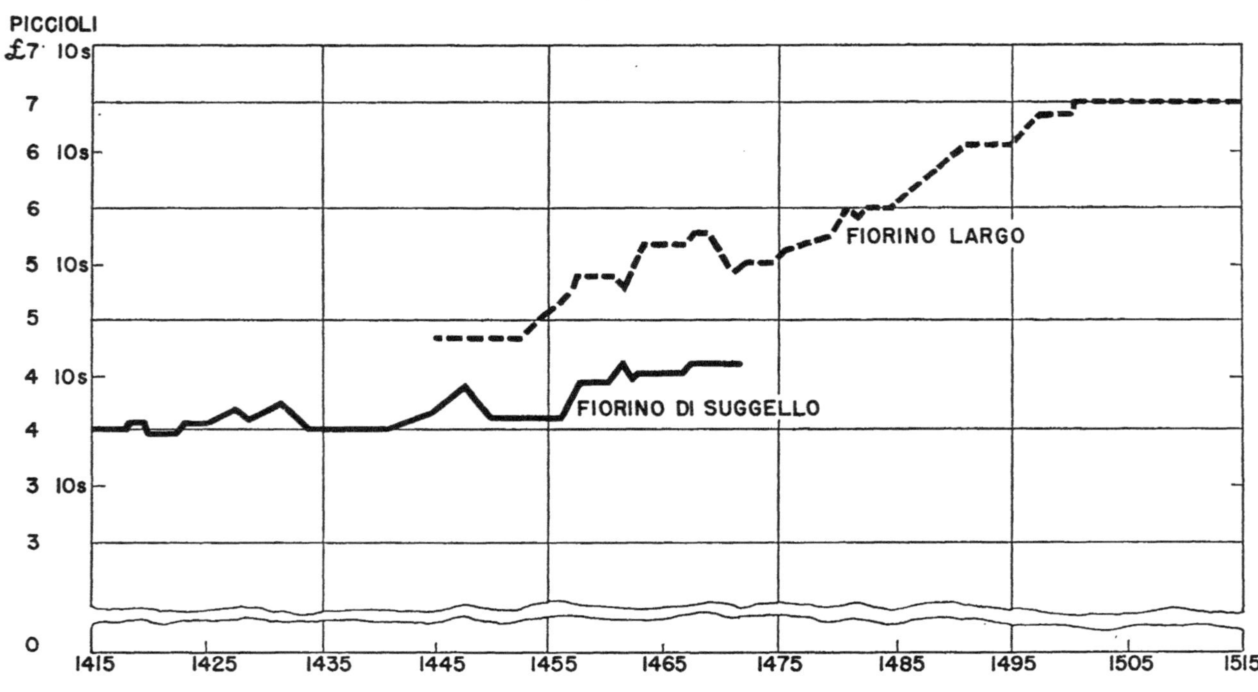

SOURCES: SELFRIDGE MEDICI MANUSCRIPTS, HARVARD BUSINESS SCHOOL.
FRANCESCO VETTORI, IL FIORINO D'ORO (FLORENCE, 1738), PP. 232-238.

drawals involved a loss of working capital that was replenished apparently by obtaining interest-bearing deposits. But this method of finance only increased the burden of interest payments at a time when profits were falling off. Risky loans to princes and the resulting capital losses further increased the strain on working capital and the danger of operating with borrowed funds. As losses piled up, working capital shrank still further. To replace it, more borrowing became necessary. Finally bankruptcy was avoided only by dipping into the state treasury. Lorenzo the Magnificent did not hesitate to salvage his bank by defrauding the Monte delle Dote, a pool or mutual fund for the payment of dowries. It is not surprising that enemies of Lorenzo have accused him of misappropriation of public funds. His admirers have tried to excuse his actions, but they have never been able to prove that the accusation is entirely without foundation.

Cracks in the structure of the Medici banking house began to appear even before the death of Cosimo. A survey of the surviving records gives decidedly the impression that, by that time, the Medici bank had passed the peak of its prosperity and was already on the decline. If Cosimo had lived, it is possible that he might have prevented the building from crumbling and that he might have taken the drastic measures which were necessary to buttress the tottering walls. But his successors did not have his business ability nor that of his younger son Giovanni di Cosimo, who died prematurely in 1463. Piero di Cosimo, the elder son, who was in poor health, had not been trained for business. Nonetheless he did much better than was expected. For a time he tried to stem the tide by adopting a policy of retrenchment. He declared that "he intended to keep what he had in substance and in credit and not to acquire more in dubious ways."[98] This conservative program was not, or could not be, carried out. Even Piero, who was bedridden most of the time, was prevailed upon by his advisers or was forced by circumstances to make decisions that were inconsistent with his program.

After Lorenzo came to the helm, matters went from bad to worse. Political considerations were given priority over cool business judgment. As Lorenzo had little interest in business, vital decisions were postponed. No farsighted policy seems to have been followed. As new cracks appeared, they were patched up, but patching up did not prevent the cracks from spreading until the entire structure was beyond

[98] Sieveking, *Handlungsbücher der Medici,* p. 50.

Courtesy of the Metropolitan Museum of Art, New York

FRANCESCO SASSETTI, GENERAL MANAGER OF THE MEDICI BANK, WITH HIS ELDEST SON, TEODORO (D. 1479)

The Workshop of Domenico Ghirlandajo

The Bache Collection, The Metropolitan Museum of Art, New York

repair. Branch managers received no guidance from above; they were left to shift for themselves.

Instead of retrenching, the Medici became more and more entangled in speculative enterprises, such as the alum cartel, or in loans to princes "which involved more risks than profits" according to Piero's prophetic words. One branch after another got into difficulties and had to be liquidated or reorganized.

The London branch came to grief before 1464, the year of Cosimo's death. The trouble originated in excessive loans to Edward IV.[99] Business conditions in England had become increasingly unfavorable to the Italians because of a concourse of circumstances: the War of the Roses, the growing hostility of the City and the English merchants toward the Italians, and the steady decline in the quantity of wool that was available for export, a result of the rapid development of the English cloth industry.[100] In order to obtain export licenses from the King, it was necessary to lend him money. And his demands never ceased. New licenses could be obtained only by granting new loans. Conditions in England were so unstable that one branch manager, Giovanni de' Bardi, gave up in despair. For a time the London branch was managed by an unreliable factor, Gherardo Canigiani, who was more interested in ingratiating himself with Edward IV than in giving faithful service to his masters.[101] Angelo Tani was sent to London in 1467 and finally succeeded in making a settlement with Edward IV which provided for the gradual extinction of the King's debt. The ink on this agreement was scarcely dry when the War of the Roses flared up again. Edward IV, after his victories at Barnet and Tewkesbury, reascended the throne of England, but he had sunk deeper into debt and was less able to pay than ever before. Many of the rebels were debtors of the Medici; they had been slain and their property was seized. The only solution was to wind up the Medici partnership in London. The liquidation dragged on for several years. In 1478 losses totaling Fl. 51,533 were written off.[102]

99 Grunzweig, *Correspondance*, pp. xxviii f.

100 Eileen Power, "The English Wool Trade in the Reign of Edward IV," *The Cambridge Historical Journal*, II (1926), 18 f.

101 Cora L. Scofield, *The Life and Reign of Edward the Fourth* (London, 1923), II, 420–28, a detailed biography of Gherardo Canigiani, unfortunately based exclusively on English sources. Canigiani never was admitted as a partner. After breaking off his connection with the Medici, he married an Englishwoman and obtained letters of denization. In English documents he is called "merchant, citizen and mercer of London, sometime of the fellowship of the Medicis of Florence, and factor and attorney of the same."

102 Sieveking, *Handlungsbücher der Medici*, p. 51.

The Medici branch in Venice disappeared before 1470.[103] No one knows why it was liquidated.

Tommaso Portinari was the captain who steered the Bruges branch onto the rocks by lending large sums to Charles the Bold. In 1478, the Medici decided to pull out and to limit their losses. The partnership with Portinari was dissolved, and Lorenzo received Fl. 16,616 in final settlement.[104] The other partners also withdrew and received their shares. This settlement left Portinari practically without working capital but with many debts and with doubtful claims on the government and the Hanseatic League.[105] Portinari spent the rest of his life prosecuting those claims and staving off creditors who were assailing him from all sides. It is not true, as several historians have written, that the Medici company in Bruges continued to do business until 1485 under the management of Pierantonio Bandini-Baroncelli.[106] This man was the Bruges manager of the Pazzi bank and never was in the service of the Medici.[107]

The Lyons branch was mismanaged by Lionetto de' Rossi, and in 1488 was on the verge of collapse. The situation was so serious that Francesco Sassetti himself rode from Florence to Lyons and stayed there a long time in order to save what could be saved. He succeeded fairly well, since the Lyons branch, together with the Rome branch and the *banco* in Florence, was still in existence when the Medici were overthrown in 1494. In consequence of this event, the business of the Lyons branch was taken over by the firm Lorenzo Tornabuoni, Cosimo Sassetti, and Lorenzo Spinelli.[108]

The *banco* in Florence also came to an end as a result of the revolution of 1494. The mob invaded the Medici palace and burned

103 "La mia ragione di Vinegia ch'è finita e più non vi tegniamo trafficho."—*Idem, Aus Genueser Rechnungs- und Steuerbüchern,* p. 101.

104 Grunzweig, *Correspondance,* p. xxxiv.

105 In an ordinance of Maximilian dated January 6, 1488 (N.S.), it is stated explicitly that Portinari was forced to give up his business because he was deprived of his capital.—L. Gilliodts-van Severen, *Cartulaire de l'ancien grand tonlieu dé Bruges* (Bruges, 1908), I, 343.

106 Sieveking, *Handlungsbücher der Medici,* p. 53; Otto Meltzing, *Das Bankhaus der Medici und siene Vorläufer* (Jena, 1906), p. 110. Although Grunzweig corrects their mistake (*Correspondance,* p. xxxiv), it is faithfully repeated by Gutkind, *Cosimo,* p. 186.

107 In Bruges documents, Pierantonio Bandini-Baroncelli is called "Pierre Antoine Banding, marchand de Florence, facteur et compaignon de la compagnie Francisque et Andrea de Pacis."—Gilliodts, *Cartulaire de l'Estaple,* II, 224, No. 1181. He was related to Tommaso Portinari's wife, Maria Bandini-Baroncelli. Pierantonio apparently continued to reside in Bruges after the Pazzi conspiracy and probably traded for his own account from 1478 onward. He was Florentine consul in 1490.—*Ibid.,* p. 270, No. 1253.

108 Harvard Graduate School of Business Administration, Selfridge Collection of Medici Manuscripts, MS 495, Section C, pp. 53–63, contains a copy of the agreement between the custodians of the Medici property and the new firm of Tornabuoni, Sassetti, and Spinelli.

most of the records.[109] All the property of Piero de' Medici and his brothers was sequestered. Custodians appointed by the new government liquidated the bank and took over the administration of the other property and the landed estates. As we have seen, there was not enough to satisfy all the creditors.

The Rome branch, which controlled a subbranch in Naples, shared in 1494 the fate of the Lyons branch. The manager, Giovanni Tornabuoni, formed a partnership with his son Lorenzo Tornabuoni and made an arrangement with the new government about the equity of the Medici in the business. Their affairs were in such bad shape that their debt exceeded their equity by Fl. 11,243. In addition, the Medici owed Fl. 7,500 charged to the account of Cardinal Giovanni de' Medici, later Pope Leo X.[110]

The Milan branch had been founded in 1450. It was housed in a magnificent palace, a gift from Francesco Sforza to Cosimo de' Medici.[111] Probably the branch paid rent for the use of this palace which was the private property of the senior partners. The records of the Medici branch in Milan have all been destroyed except for a small fragment of the ledger in use during the year 1459. The branch was still prosperous in 1478, when Lorenzo was able to draw on its reserves during the crisis which followed the Pazzi conspiracy. Up to 1468, its manager at Milan was Pigello Portinari, Tommaso's brother. When he died during that year, he was succeeded by another brother, Accerito. Because of the clever management of Pigello and Accerito Portinari, the Milan branch apparently never got into trouble. Perhaps it was liquidated to cover losses elsewhere. In any case it had ceased to exist by 1494.

According to the testimony of Philippe de Commines, the Medici bank was the largest banking house in existence in his time.[112] It had seven or eight branches and employed from forty to fifty factors, not including the branch managers who were junior partners and not employees. Besides the factors who served the Medici bank abroad,

[109] Black stains can still be seen on the few records and fragments which were saved from the flames.

[110] Selfridge Collection, MS 495, Section C, pp. 17–37, contains the agreement between the custodians and the Tornabuoni.

[111] This palace was considerably enlarged and embellished by Cosimo. A description of the building is given by Antonio Averlino Filarete, *Tractat über die Baukunst nebst seinen Büchern von der Zeichenkunst und den Bauten der Medici,* ed. Wolfgang von Oettingen (Vienna, 1890), pp. 679–86. Cf. Alfred Gotthold Meyer, *Oberitalienische Frührenaissance, Bauten und Bildwerke der Lombardei* (Berlin, 1897), I, 99–110.

[112] Philippe de Commynes, *Mémoires,* eds. Joseph Calmette et G. Durville (Paris, 1925), Vol. III, Book VI, chap. vii, p. 41.

there were several *discepoli* or clerks in Florence, perhaps ten or twelve. Compared with the size of modern corporations, these figures are not impressive, but the Medici bank was a giant for its time. It may even be argued that it was too large. It is possible that, as deposits poured in, it became increasingly difficult to find suitable investments for loanable funds. Investment opportunities were practically restricted to foreign trade and to the business of exchange. Rather than refuse deposits, the Medici succumbed to the temptation of seeking an outlet for surplus cash in making dangerous loans to princes. This policy proved to be their undoing as it had caused the ruin of the Peruzzi in the fourteenth century and later brought the Fuggers to the brink of bankruptcy. It seems that it was a general weakness of what N. S. B. Gras has called "the financial type of sedentary merchant" to drift from private banking into government finance.[113] Nearly always the results were catastrophic. The case of the Medici is no exception to the general rule.

[113] Gras, *Business and Capitalism*, p. 166.

I. SHARE OF FRANCESCO SASSETTI IN THE GENEVA BRANCH OF THE MEDICI BANK

The account given in Table 1 is an excerpt from the private account book of Francesco Sassetti, the *ministro* or general manager of the Medici, and reveals that he had ∇2,300 (of 64 *scudi* to the gold mark) invested in the capital of the Medici branch in Geneva. According to the entry on the debit side of the account,

TABLE 1

ACCOUNT OF THE MEDICI BRANCH IN GENEVA CONCERNING SASSETTI'S SHARE IN THE CAPITAL

Debit Side

Explanation	Amount in Scudi Vecchi			Amount in Fiorini di Suggello		
1462	∇	*s.*	*d.*	F.	*s.*	*d.*
La compangnia et trafficho di Ginevra che dice in Francesco Sassetti e compagnia dè dare ∇2,300 vecchi levati in dì primo di novembre dal libro paonazzo da carta 96 per lo corpo debbo tenere in ditta ragione dove participo pel ¼ e i Medici per la ½ et Francesco Nori et Giuliano del Zaccheria per lo ¼ com' appare per la schritta che chominciò detta compagnia a dì 26 di marzo 1461, posto in questo a carta 2..........	2,300	0	0	2,576	0	0
	2,300	0	0	2,576	0	0

Credit Side

Explanation	Amount in Scudi Vecchi			Amount in Fiorini di Suggello		
1462	∇	*s.*	*d.*	F.	*s.*	*d.*
La compagnia et traffico di Ginevra scripto di contro dè avere a dì 24 di marzo 1465 ∇ottocento vecchi scrivemo loro ci facessono debitore a questo conto et creditore a quello del diposito posto debbino dare in questo a carta 12 per rifare il corpo alla ragione nuova di ∇1,500................	800	0	0	900	0	0
Et in dì primo di dicembre 1468 ∇1,500 fecion buoni per me alla ragione nuova di Giuliano del Zaccheria, posto debbi dare di sotto in questo a carta 13................	1,500	0	0	1,676	0	0
	2,300	0	0	2,576	0	0

Source: Florence, Archivio di Stato, Carte Strozziane, Series II, No. 20: Libro segreto di Francesco Sassetti, 1462–1472, fol. 13.

the capital *(corpo)* of the Geneva branch amounted to ▽9,200, of which the Medici supplied one half, or ▽4,600; Francesco Sassetti, one fourth, or ▽2,300; and Francesco Nori and Giuliano Zaccheria jointly, another fourth, or ▽2,300. Incidentally, this is the Francesco Nori who was slain beside Giuliano de' Medici in the Cathedral of Florence on the fateful day of the Pazzi conspiracy (1478). By that time he had probably been promoted from branch manager to assistant manager of the main bank in Florence.

According to the first entry on the credit side of the account, the capital of the Geneva branch was reduced from ▽9,200 to ▽6,000 on March 24, 1466, when the Geneva branch was moved to Lyons. As a result, Sassetti's share in the capital was brought down to ▽1,500, and ▽800 were transferred from his *corpo* or capital account to his *deposito* or deposit account. The second entry on the credit side apparently refers to a renewal of the partnership agreement on December 1, 1468. The account is closed, and the sum of ▽1,500 is charged to the *ragione nuova* or new partnership.

II. DIVISION OF PROFITS AMONG THE PARTNERS OF THE LYONS BRANCH

This account, reproduced in Table 2, also taken from Sassetti's private account book, relates to the division of the profits of the Lyons branch. These profits apparently amounted to ▽8,493 17*s.* 6*d.* for the year 1466 and were divided among the partners as follows:

Piero de' Medici...........	8*s.* 0*d.* in the £	▽3,397 11*s.* 0 *d.*
Giuliano Zaccheria........	3*s.* 4*d.* in the £	1,415 12*s.* 11 *d.*
Francesco Nori............	4*s.* 4*d.* in the £	1,840 6*s.* 9½*d.*
Francesco Sassetti..........	4*s.* 4*d.* in the £	1,840 6*s.* 9½*d.*
Total	20*s.* 0*d.* in the £	▽8,493 17*s.* 6 *d.*

These figures do not correspond exactly with those given by Francesco Sassetti because of slight carelessness on his part in computing the shares. The differences are, however, so small as to be negligible.

The profits in 1467 were less than those of the preceding year and amounted to only ▽4,855 17*s.* 5*d.*, to which were added ▽719 8*s.* 6*d.* taken from a reserve which had accumulated in previous years. The total of ▽5,575 5*s.* 11*d.* was not divided but was set aside as a reserve for bad debts, unpaid salaries and expenses, and other unforeseen contingencies. This is one of the earliest examples of accrual accounting with which I am acquainted. There are several other examples in Sassetti's account book.

At the end of the following year, 1468, ▽3,442 9*s.* 1*d.* of this reserve were actually used to meet deferred claims and to settle unpaid expenses. The balance of ▽2,132 16*s.* 10*d.* was left in the Reserve Account.

TABLE 2

Account Relating to the Division of Profits Among the Partners of the Lyons Branch

Debit Side

Explanation	Amount in Scudi di 64 al Marco			Amount in Fiorini di Suggello		
	∇	*s.*	*d.*	F.	*s.*	*d.*
1467 La raxone di Lione che dice in Francesco Sassetti e compania dè dare ∇8,493 *s.*17½ a oro di 64 che tanto montorono gl' avanzi di detta raxone dell'anno 1466 come appare pe' conti ce ne mandorono saldi i quali attengono a tutti i compagni posto avanzi debbino avere di sotto a carta 24........	8,493	17	6	9,513	0	0
Et per gli avanzi dell'anno 1467 ∇4,855 *s.*17 *d.* 5 et più ∇719 *s.*8 *d.*6 di quali aveano creditore uno riservo in tutto ∇5,575 *s.*5 *d.*11 fecion creditore Avanzi et riservi posto debbino avere di sotto a carta 24....	5,575	5	11	6,237	0	0
	14,069	3	5	15,750	0	0

Credit Side

Explanation	Amount in Scudi di 64 al Marco			Amount in Fiorini di Suggello		
	∇	*s.*	*d.*	F.	*s.*	*d.*
1467 La Raxone di Lione schritta dirimpetto de avere ∇6,653. 2. 7. a oro di 64 fecion buoni ∇3,397 *s.*7 a Piero di Cosimo, e ∇1,840. 4. 7 a Francesco Nori, e ∇1,415. 11. 3 a Giuliano Zaccheria per la loro parte di ∇8,493.17.6 che in dì 26 di marzo 1468 partirono degl' avanzi di detta raxone posto debbino dare di sotto a carta 24, cioè a Piero di Cosimo a raxone di soldi 8 per lira, a Francesco Nori a raxone di soldi 4 denari 4 per lira, a Giuliano Zaccheria a raxone di soldi 3 denari 4 per lira in tutto come si dice ∇6,653. 2. 7.....................	6,653	12	11	7,451	0	0
E a noi per la nostra parte a raxone di soldi 4 denari 4 per lira ∇1,840 *s.*4 *d.*7 posto debbino dare a altro loro conto in questo a carta 22.......................	1,840	4	7	2,062	0	0
E posto disavanzi debbino dare di sotto carta 24 che tanti meno che li ∇5,575 soldi 5 [den. 11] dirimpetto feciono, restassino detti avanzi per spese e salari o altro com' appare pe' conti mandato in saldi in dì primo dicembre 1468 di mano di Giuliano..	3,442	9	1	3,852	0	0
E posto disavanzi sopradetti debbino dare di sotto a carta 24 perchè li lasciamo alla ragione nuova che dice in Lorenzo de' Medici e Francesco Sassetti che cominciò l'anno 1470 e a loro n'ànno assegnati conto e mescolati con loro....................	2,132	16	10	2,385	0	0
	14,069	3	5	15,750	0	0

Source: Libro segreto di Francesco Sassetti, fol. 24.

III. DEPOSITS OF FRANCESCO SASSETTI WITH SEVERAL BRANCHES

Table 3 gives the text of an account relating to a time deposit of Fl. 5,000 *larghi* or Fl. 6,000 *di suggello* which was invested in the *sopracorpo* of the Milan branch, when Sassetti made an inventory of his estate on November 1, 1462. The interest *(discrezione, provedigione)* on this deposit was apparently 10 per cent. At the end of the calendar year 1463, Florentine style, or March 24, 1464 (N.S.), Sassetti received Fl. 500 *larghi* interest which was compounded and added to the principal. As he deposited another Fl. 500, in cash, these two transactions increased the balance to Fl. 6,000 *larghi*. The interest in the two following years was paid out and not compounded. In 1467, Sassetti withdrew a total of Fl. 2,600 *larghi*, or Fl. 2,000 of the principal plus Fl. 600 interest. The balance was thus brought down to Fl. 4,000. During the next two years, 1467 and 1468, Sassetti received only Fl. 400 or 10 per cent on Fl. 4,000. The entire sum was withdrawn on June 10, 1469.

Perhaps it should be pointed out that Sassetti made an additional profit of Fl. 107 *di suggello* because of the rise in value of the *fiorino largo* or large florin. This item is transferred to Profit and Loss. As already explained, the steady appreciation of the *fiorino largo* benefited the depositor but added to the burden assumed by the Medici bank. The entries in Sassetti's account book fully confirm the correctness of this analysis.

Sometimes Sassetti deposited money with one of the branches, not in his own name but in that of a third party who might or might not have known anything about the transaction. There are at least two examples of this deceptive practice in Sassetti's account book. The first instance concerns a deposit of Fl. 16,249 1*s*. 2*d*. *pitetti* with the Medici branch in Avignon. This money apparently belonged to Sassetti but the deposit was made in the name of the Monastery of the Celestines. In other words, the sum of Fl. 16,249 1*s*. 2*d*. *pitetti* was written to the credit of the Monastery in the books of the Avignon branch, although the money was probably Sassetti's.[1] So far as I have been able to make out from the entries in the account book, the Celestine monks had no interest whatsoever in this deposit. The other case relates to a deposit of ∇5,000 with the Lyons branch. According to Sassetti's entries, this money was left by him on deposit at the discretion of the Lyons branch, but was written not to his credit but to that of one Ami di Pemes in the secret ledger of the said branch.[2]

Why were deposits written to the credit of straw men concealing the name of the actual depositor? The answer to this question can be only tentative. Sassetti was a partner, both in the Avignon and in the Lyons branches, and as such his responsibility was unlimited. In case of bankruptcy, all his investments, his

[1] Libro segreto di Francesco Sassetti, fol. 38^{v}: "Giovanni Zampini e compagnia di Vingnone per uno conto di danari tenghono *di mio* in diposito in nome del Convento de' Cilestrini deono dare Fiorini 16,249 s.1 d.2 di Vignone, posto debbino avere in questo a carta 31 per resto di quel conto d'accordo con loro, messo ongni provexione e discretione fino a tutto l'anno 1471. . . . Fl. 16,249.1.2 *pitetti;* Fl. 7,285 *larghi* [italics mine]."

[2] *Ibid.*, fol. 22^{r}: "Francesco Sassetti e compagnia di Lione deono dare ∇5,000 di 64 al marco, posto debbino avere in questo a carta 12 a altro loro conto vecchio adietro, i quali lasciò loro in diposito al loro discretione cominciando a dì 26 di marzo 1467.. ∇5,000, F. 5,750 di suggello. Annomene creditore al loro libro segreto paonazzo a carta 8 in nome di Ami di Pemes."

deposits as well as his shares in the capital, were liable to seizure by the creditors. Perhaps the use of straw men was a precaution designed to defraud the creditors in case of failure. In such an eventuality, the stratagem would have enabled Sassetti not only to evade his responsibility but to lay claim to the assets as a general creditor and to share in the distribution of any liquidation dividends.

TABLE 3

ACCOUNT OF THE MILAN BRANCH CONCERNING A TIME DEPOSIT

Made by Francesco Sassetti

Debit Side

Explanation	Amount in Fiorini Larghi			Amount in Fiorini di Suggello		
1462	F	s.	d.	F.	s.	d.
Piero et Johanni de'Medici e compagnia di Milano deono dare fiorini cinquemila larghi di Firenze levati in dì primo di Novembre dall'altro libro paonazzo carta 80 i quali mi restarono a dare sino a dì 24 di marzo passato d'accordo con loro et tengonli in diposito a lloro discretione posti a Valsente a carta 2..............................	5,000	0	0	6,000	0	0
E deono dare fiorini cinquecento larghi per discretione de' detti danari insino a tutto l'anno 1463 d'accordo con loro posti in questo a carta 20.....................	500	0	0	600	0	0
E a dì 22 di maggio fiorini cinquecento larghi per loro a'Medici di Firenze come ordinò Pigello [Portinari] paghoronli i miei dall'altro libro azurro et missonli a mio conto a detto libro a carta 50 posto Francesco Sassetti per denari contanti debbi avere a carta 19............................	500	0	0	600	0	0
E deono dare fiorini secento larghi per provixione di detti fiorini 6,000 larghi tenuti in diposito a loro discretione fino a tutto l'anno 1464 posti in questo a carta 20......	600	0	0	726	0	0
E deono dare fiorini secento larghi per providigione di detti denari fino a tutto il '65 a lloro discretione d'accordo, posti in questo a carta 20.....................	600	0	0	730	0	0
E per provedigione di detti denari fino a tutto l'anno 1466 d'accordo con loro, posti in questo a carta 20...................	600	0	0	750	0	0
E per provedigione di f.4,000 larghi restanno a dare a questo conto fino a tutto l'anno 1467, posto avanzi debbino avere in questo a carta 20.....................	400	0	0	488	0	0
E per providigione di f.4,000 larghi restavano a dare di questo conto fino a tutto l'anno 1468, posto avanzi debbino avere in questo a carta 20.....................	400	0	0	486	0	0
E posto avanzi debbino avere in questo carta 20 per resto di qui avanzati nel ragione a mi conto di fiorini larghi.............				107	0	8
	8,600	0	0	10,487	0	8

TABLE 3

Account of the Milan Branch Concerning a Time Deposit

Made by Francesco Sassetti
Credit Side

Explanation	Amount in Fiorini Larghi			Amount in Fiorini di Suggello		
1462	F	*s.*	*d.*	F.	*s.*	*d.*
Piero et Johanni de'Medici e compagnia di Milano deono avere a dì 3 di luglo 1465 fiorini secento larghi i quali ci mandorono contanti et ebbonli i nostri dell'altro libro che tiene Luigi Ghuidotti che s'achonciano per contanti in questo a carta 19...........	600	0	0	726	0	0
E a dì 27 di giungno 1466 fiorini secento larghi feciono buoni per me a'nostri di Lione et io gl'ebbi da lloro contanti qui in Firenze com' appare a lloro conto al libro nostro azurro che tiene Luigi a carta 179, posto a mio conto a carta 19...................	600	0	0	736	10	0
E a dì 22 d'aprile 1467 fiorini milletrecento larghi i quali mi mandorono contanti per Francesco Nori et per me ai nostri di qui, posto debbino dare al libro paonazzo a carta 136 e a mio conto per contanti in questo a carta 19.....................	1,300	0	0	1,629	6	8
E a dì 23 detto fiorini 1,080 larghi fecionmi buoni per loro i nostri di Lione e per li detti i nostri da qui, posto debbino dare al libro paonazzo a carta 136 e a mio conto per contanti in questo a carta 19...........	1,080	0	0	1,350	0	0
E a dì detto fiorini 220 larghi fecionmi buoni i detti di Lione e per loro i nostri di qui, posto debbino dare al libro paonazzo a carta 136 e a mio conto per contanti in questo a carta 19.....................	220	0	0	275	0	0
E dì 26 d'aprile 1468 fiorini quattrocento larghi mandoronomi contanti in uno legato questo dì per Valentino Corner [illegible], Francesco Sassettti posto debbi dare a carta 19.............................	400	0	0	488	0	0
E a dì 10 di giungno 1469 fiorini 4,400 larghi per loro da'nostri dell'altro libro che tiene Luigi Guidotti a chui li mandorono contanti in maggior somma e fecionme ne creditore al libro grande bianco a carta 35 e Io ne li feci debitore all'altro mio libro paonazzo a carta 159 e mio conto per contanti a carta 19...................	4,400	0	0	5,282	4	0
	8,600	0	0	10,487	0	8

Source: Libro segreto di Francesco Sassetti, fol. 11.

IV. *NOSTRO* ACCOUNT OF THE VENETIAN BRANCH OF THE MEDICI BANK IN THE BOOKS OF THE BRUGES BRANCH

The first entry on the debit side of this account (Table 4) relates to an interesting transaction in triangular exchange involving three different currencies and three Medici branches: (1) the Medici branch in Venice; (2) the one in Bruges; and (3) the one in Geneva (Switzerland), managed by Amerigo Benci. Apparently, Benci informed Bruges that, on May 13, 1441, he had requested the Venetian branch to debit the Geneva branch and to credit the Bruges branch for an amount of 660 Venetian ducats or £66 *di grossi in oro*. This amount was the equivalent of 10 gold marks at 66 ducats per mark or of 640 écus of 64 to the gold mark. On the basis of this information, the Bruges branch, on June 20, 1441, debited the *Nostro* account of the Venetian branch with 660 ducats or £66 *di grossi in oro,* Venetian currency, worth £140 groat in Flemish currency, and credited the Geneva branch with 640 écus, which were also worth £140 groat at 52½ groats per écu of 64 to the mark. The result of this transaction was that the Bruges bank now had 660 ducats more standing to its credit in Venice, but that, on the other hand, there were 640 écus less to its credit in Geneva.

At that time, accounts in Geneva were kept in écus of 64 to the gold mark. This relation was fixed. The exchange rates were based either on the mark or on the écu of 64. According to the above transaction, the equivalence, or parity, between the three currencies involved was as follows:

1 gold mark of 64 écus = 66 ducats
1 écu of 64 to the mark = 52½ groats
1 Venetian ducat = about 51 groats

This latter figure was slightly below the actual rate of the ducat in Bruges at that particular time. This transaction was consequently profitable to the Bruges branch, since it acquired ducats at a cheaper rate than it was possible to buy them directly in Bruges.

It should perhaps be emphasized that money was transferred from Bruges to Venice via Geneva by simple book transfer. Specie does not come into the picture at all. The case is an excellent illustration to show how specie was entirely eliminated in the making of international payments.

The next entry on the debit side refers to a three-cornered exchange transaction of the same kind, but involving Barcelona, Bruges, and Venice. Apparently, the firm Giovanni Ventura and Co., the Medici correspondents in Barcelona, sent a remittance of 152⅜ ducats to Venice. The Medici in Venice were to collect this remittance from Giovanni de' Prioli on August 26, 1441, and to credit the Bruges branch with the proceeds. The ducat was rated in Barcelona at 15*s.* 9*d.*, Barcelonese currency. Ventura charged the account of the Bruges branch with ▽355 plus 12 groats as the price of this remittance. These écus were moneys of account having a fixed value of 22 groats. The exchange rate was 6*s.* 9*d.*, Barcelonese currency per écu (▽). Between Barcelona and Bruges, the exchange rate was always based upon the écu of 22 groats. Upon receipt of Ventura's letter, the Bruges branch of the Medici bank accordingly debited the Venetian branch with

152⅜ ducats, or £15 4*s.* 9*d. di grossi in oro,* and credited Ventura with £32 11*s.* 10*d.* groat, or ▽355 of 22 groats plus 12 odd groats.

These figures give the following equations:

152⅜ Venetian ducats at 24 *grossi* per ducat = £15 4*s.* 9*d. di grossi*
152⅜ Venetian ducats at 15*s.* 9*d.* Barcel. per ducat = £119 19*s.* 11*d.* Barcel.
£119 19*s.* 11*d.* Barcelonese at 6*s.* 9*d.* Barcel. per écu = ▽$355\frac{12}{22}$
▽355 and 12 groats at 22 groats per ▽ = £32 11*s.* 10*d.* groat
152⅜ ducats = £15 4*s.* 9*d. di grossi in oro* = £32 11*s.* 10*d.* groat

The last equation gives approximately 51 groats as the value of the ducat in Bruges. This value corresponded more or less to the actual rate of the ducat in Bruges, as appears from other entries in the ledger.

Apparently the balance of trade between Bruges and Barcelona was usually favorable to Bruges, that between Bruges and Venice was usually favorable to Venice, and that between Barcelona and Venice was usually favorable to Barcelona. In any case, the Bruges merchant bankers often had credit balances accumulating in Barcelona and payments to make in Venice. In order to pay the Venetians, the Bruges bankers were glad to use their balances in Catalonia either to buy claims on Venice in Barcelona or to sell drafts on Barcelona in Venice. The entries in the Medici ledger date from 1441. This evidence concerning the trade relations of Bruges, Venice, and Barcelona is strengthened by the fact that the same method of settling international balances was used fifty years earlier by merchant bankers in Bruges, as we know from their letters to the office in Barcelona of Francesco Datini and Co. Already at that time, the Italian bankers in Bruges were using their credits in Catalonia to transfer funds to Venice.

The next entry on the debit side refers to an exchange transaction of the conventional type. According to this entry, the Bruges branch of the Medici remitted 500 ducats to the Venetian bank. This remittance was in the form of a draft payable by Cecco di Tomaso and Brothers in Venice and purchased from Bernardo Cambi and Co. in Bruges at the rate of 52⅞ groats per ducat or at a total price of £110 3*s.* 1*d.* groat.

The succeeding entry also refers to an exchange transaction of the usual type. This one involved the Medici branch in Bruges as remitter, the Medici branch in Venice as payee, Guglielmo da Casasaggia in Venice as payor, and Bartolomeo Riba, a Catalan in Bruges, as drawer or taker. The face value of the bill of exchange was 100 ducats. It was bought by the Medici of Bruges at the rate of 52⅚ groats per ducat.

The last entry on the debit side refers to a balance of £959 6*s.* 6½*d. di grossi,* Venetian currency, or £1,980 3*s.* 6*d.* groat, Flemish currency, carried over from a previous account. Probably this transfer was made after receiving a statement from Venice.

The first entry on the credit side relates to the sale of a draft on Venice to a Bruges grocer. The draft, which amounted to only 40 ducats, was sold at the rate of 53 groats per ducat. After an entry concerning the purchase of pepper, there is another concerning a transfer from the account of the Medici bank in Venice to the debit of the branch in Rome.

The fourth entry is exceedingly interesting because it deals with a protested bill of exchange which was returned unpaid by the Venetian branch of the Medici bank. This branch is credited with 230 ducats, the face value of the bill, plus one-half ducat for protest fees. The bill had been bought from Paolo Bociardo—probably a Fleming named Bosschaert, since Bociardo does not sound very Italian—at the exchange rate of 49 groats per ducat. Since the payor in Venice had failed to pay the bill at maturity, recourse was taken against the drawer and he was made to pay the 230½ ducats, not at the original rate of 49 groats per ducat but at that of 54 groats, the exchange rate prevailing in Venice when the bill fell due. The drawer who was ultimately responsible for the payment of the bill thus lost 5 groats per ducat on the exchange. As already explained, the ducat was usually rated higher in Venice than in Bruges, but in this case a rising exchange added much to the burden of the unfortunate drawer. He had originally received 230 ducats at 49 groats per ducat, or £46 19*s.* 2*d.* groat. The total loss was £4 18*s.* 1*d.* groat, or 230 times 5 groats plus 27 groats (one-half ducat) for protest charges.

This was a loss of more than 10 per cent over a period of three or four months. The loss was evidently so high because the exchange had risen from 49 to 51 or 52 groats in Bruges and even higher in Venice, while the bill traveled to Venice and back to Bruges. Instead of the drawer losing, the Medici might have lost, if the exchange had gone down rather than up. As explained before, the business of exchange was speculative and profits or losses were uncertain and unpredictable. The presence of the interest factor, however, favored the lender to the detriment of the borrower.

The next entry of interest concerns the purchase of 100 *chariche* of pepper bought by the Venetian branch for the account of the Bruges branch. These 100 *chariche* of pepper were to be shipped from Venice to Bruges on the Venetian galleys, but only 54 *chariche* were taken aboard for lack of space. Another lot of pepper was bought jointly by the two Medici branches. Each had a half interest in the venture.

There are on the credit side several entries concerning remittances sent by the Venetian branch. One of these remittances was a bill of 400 ducats drawn by Marino Barbo in Venice on Marco Corner in Bruges. Another remittance was a bill drawn by Andrea Monaldi in Venice on Giovanni Arnolfini in Bruges. Each of these transactions involved two payments and four persons: an advance of funds made by the Medici of Venice to a merchant residing there and the repayment of this loan in Bruges by a correspondent of this merchant to the local branch of the Medici bank.

The last entry on the credit side is the transfer of the balance to another folio of the ledger. This entry shows that the Bruges branch of the Medici bank had about 4,176 ducats standing to its credit in Venice on September 30, 1441.

By way of conclusion, it should perhaps be pointed out that most drafts or remittances were made out in amounts of 100, 200, 300, 400, or 500 ducats. This prevalence of round figures is, in my opinion, very significant. It underlines the financial character of the Medieval exchange business. Contrary to the general belief, the great majority of Medieval bills were finance bills, that is, they were based on loans and not on bona fide commercial transactions. Other bills were issued to adjust international balances. The Medici account books show plainly that the movement of bills was far greater than the volume of international trade. Other account books of merchant bankers, for example, those of Francesco Datini or Filippo Borromei, reveal the same fact. It is likely, therefore, that a considerable volume of local trade was financed by the sale of international bills.

TABLE 4

Nostro Account of the Venetian Branch of the Medici Bank in the Ledger of the Bruges Branch

Debit Side

Explanation	Venetian Currency Lire di grossi			Flemish Currency Pounds groat		
1441	£	s.	d.	£	s.	d.
Chosimo de' Medici e conpagnia di Vinegia per nostro chonto là deono dare a dì 20 di giugnio £ sessantasei di grossi sono per la valuta di ducati 660 avisorono e' Benci di Ginevra per loro lettera di dì 13 di maggio avere scripto a detti che per dì 30 detto cene faciano creditore e lloro debitore per marchi 10 d'oro a ducati 66 per marco chonti alloro medesimi i quali ragioniamo a grossi 52½ per scudo di 64 montano lire cientoquaranta di grossi [moneta di Fiandra] posto detto Benci deono avere in questo a carta 201....	66	0	0	140	0	0
Several items omitted..................	193	6	0	417	2	11
E dì detto [27 Luglio] £ quindici s. quattro d. nove di grossi sono per la valuta di ducati 152⅜ avisorono detti di Barzalona per detta loro lettera aver loro per noi rimesso da Giovanni de' Prioli per loro lettera per la valuta a s.15 d. 9 [barzalonesi] per ducato chonti alloro medesimi a dì 7 per dì 26 d'aghosto i quali ragioniamo a s.6 d.9 [barzalonesi] per scudo, sono scudi 355 grossi 12, vagliono a grossi 22 per scudo £ trentadue s. undici d. dieci di grossi	15	4	9	32	11	10
One item omitted......................	5	0	0	10	9	4
E dì 2 d'aghosto £ cinquanta di grossi sono per la valuta di ducati 500 auto loro detto dì per uso da Ceccho di Tomaso e fratelli chambiare chon Bernardo Chambi e Co. a grossi 52⅞ per ducato montano £ ciento dieci s.tre d. uno di grossi, posto detto Bernardo dè avere in questo a carta 209	50	0	0	110	3	1
E dì 5 detto £ dieci di grossi sono per la valuta di ducati 100 rimettemo loro detto dì pèr uso da Ghuglielmo da Chasasaggia chambiare chon Bartolomeo Riba a grossi 52⅚ per ducato in somma di ducati 300 montano £ ventidue s.— d.tre di grossi, posto detto dè avere in somma di £ 66 d. 10 di grossi in questo a carta 256........	10	0	0	22	0	3
E dì 18 detto £ novecientocinquantanove s. sei d. sei ½ di grossi che restanno in £ millenoveciento-ottanta s. tre d. sei di grossi posto deono avere in questo carta 195 per resto di quello chonto.................	959	6	6½	1,980	3	6
One item omitted......................	2	0	0	4	6	4
	1,300	17	3½	2,716	17	3

TABLE 4

Nostro Account of the Venetian Branch of the Medici Bank in the Ledger of the Bruges Branch

Credit Side

Explanation	Venetian Currency Lire di grossi			Flemish Currency Pounds groat		
1441	£	*s.*	*d.*	£	*s.*	*d.*
Chosimo de' Medici e conpagnia di Venegia per nostro chonto là deono avere a dì 5 di luglio £ quattro di grossi sono per la valuta di ducati 40 traemo loro detto dì per uso in Niccolo Ulivotto per la valuta a grossi 53 per ducato avuta da Lorenzo Scharmere, speziere di Bruggia, vagliono £ otto s.sedici d.otto di grossi a entrata carta 34 posto la chasa dè dare in questo a carta 255..............	4	0	0	8	16	8
Two items omitted....................	52	10	0	113	6	8
E dì 14 detto £ ventitre s.uno di grossi sono per la valuta di ducati 230 rimettemo loro fino a dì 14 di marzo da Bernardo Zanni dare a Polo Bociardo a grossi 49 di ducato el quale no lli paghò e tornorono chol protesto a grossi 54 per ducato e più ducato ½ per lo protesto montano £ cinquantuno s.diciasette d.tre di grossi, posto detto Paolo dè dare in questo a carta 207	23	1	0	51	17	3
Two items omitted....................	44	1	0	98	17	3
E dì detto [7 d'aghosto] £ treciento ottantotto s.nove d.tre di grossi sono per chosto di chariche 100 di pepe fatte loro chonperare per nostro chonto chon ordine cie lo mandassino per le ghalee viniziane di che ci ànno detto chonto chon ispese e tutto e più di chariche 54 non ce poterono charichare a dette ghalee i quali ragioniamo a grossi 50 per ducato montano £ ottocientonove s. sei di grossi posto pepe fatto chonperare per nostro chonto dè dare in questo a carta 262......................	388	9	3	809	6	0
E dì 19 detto £114 s.7 d.6 di grossi sono per chosto di lb. 12,097 di pepe chonprato a metà per loro e noi per la nostra parte di che ci ànno detto chonto sono ducati 1,143¾ vagliono a grossi 52 per ducato £247, s.16 d.3 di grossi posto detto pepe dè dare in questo a carta 277...	114	7	6	247	16	3
Several items omitted.................	256	16	4	574	1	2
E dì 30 detto [settenbre] £417 s.12 d.2½ che ci restanno in £812 s.16 di grossi posto deono dare in questo a carta 294 per resto di questo chonto.................	417	12	2½	812	16	0
	1,300	17	3½	2,716	17	3

Source: Florence, Archivio di Stato, Mediceo avanti il Principato, filza 134, No. 2, Ledger of the Bruges branch, 1441, fol. 250.

V. *VOSTRO* OR *LORO* ACCOUNT OF THE VENETIAN BRANCH OF THE MEDICI BANK IN THE BOOKS OF THE BRUGES BRANCH

In contrast to the *Nostro* account, which has two extension columns, one for foreign currency (Venetian pounds *di grossi in oro*) and one for local currency (Flemish pounds groat), the *Vostro* account has only a column for local money. The *Vostro* account was used to record all exchange and other transactions in which the Bruges branch of the Medici bank was merely the agent of the Venetian branch. The first item on the credit side of the *Vostro* account represents the balance in Flemish currency which was owed by the Bruges branch to the Venetian branch.

The second entry on the credit side relates to a transfer from the *Nostro* to the *Vostro* account in accordance with the instructions given by the Venetian branch. The result was that 500 ducats were added to the credit of the Bruges branch in Venice and £108 *6s. 8d.* groat were also added to the credit of the Venetian branch in Bruges. The transfer was apparently made because the Bruges branch was 500 ducats short for making payments in Venice.

The next entry, of £79 *7s. 11d.* groat, is canceled by a debit entry of like amount. Anticipating a rise of the exchange, the Medici of Venice apparently sold Flemish currency at 51½ groats to Piero Horco with the understanding that they would repurchase it at usance, that is to say, at the rate prevailing in Bruges after two months. As the exchange actually rose in Bruges to 52 groats, the Medici made a profit of 3 ducats 13½ *grossi* besides having the use of the money during four months. This transaction shows that the borrower sometimes gained at the expense of the lender.

The other credit entries with one exception, another item concerning an unpaid bill returned from Venice after being protested, all relate to bills sent to Bruges for collection. For example, on June 27, 1441, the Venetian branch of the Medici bank was credited by the Bruges branch with £65 *7s. 5d.* groat in connection with a bill drawn by Piero Guidaccioni in Venice on Bernardo Cambi in Bruges. According to the entry, the face value of the bill was 301 ducats 17 *grossi* at 52 groats, or £65 *7s. 5d.* groat. As this bill probably originated in a loan made by the Venetian branch with its own funds, the sum of £65 *7s. 5d.* was posted to the credit of the *Vostro,* and not of the *Nostro* account. In other words, this is a case in which the Bruges branch owed a certain sum in Flemish currency and not in ducats to the Venetian branch. Profits or losses arising from this exchange transaction went to the Venetian branch, and the Bruges branch acting simply as collecting agent had no part in them.

On July 6 there is another entry relating to a transaction of the same sort. This time the drawer was Piero Soranzo of Venice, and the payor, the Lucchese merchant, Giusfredo Rapondi, in Bruges.

Most of the entries on the debit side of the *Vostro* account of the Venetian branch refer to bills remitted by the Bruges branch. The great number of remittances proves that the Medici were not usually borrowers but lenders who bought the drafts of lesser merchants in need of funds.

The first entry on the debit side deals with a remittance of 300 ducats, equivalent to £65 groat, payable by Guglielmo da Casassaggia in Venice and bought from Bartolomeo Riba in Bruges at the exchange rate of 52 groats.

The second entry is the counterpart of a credit entry of £79 7*s*. 11*d*. groat. As already stated, this entry involves a speculation on the rise of the ducat.

The third entry is rather interesting. It concerns a remittance payable at the August fair in Geneva. The Bruges branch apparently bought a bill of ▽419 of 66 to the mark from Marco Corner in Bruges and paid 50½ groats per ▽, or a total of £88 3*s*. 4*d*. groat. This bill was payable by Giorgio Corner in Geneva to the Medici branch in that city. However, instructions were given to this branch to credit Venice and not Bruges. There are several more entries of the same kind. Apparently the Bruges branch had its credit balances in Geneva transferred to the Venetian branch which, probably, preferred credits in Geneva to credits in Bruges.

There are many more items concerning remittances and two small items relating to protest charges in Bruges. In one case the Medici of Bruges asked a notary to protest a bill drawn upon themselves because the drawer, Niccolo di Bartolomeo, did not have sufficient funds standing to his credit in their books. The bill was apparently payable *a noi medesimi*, that is, by transfer in the books of the Bruges branch.

The *Vostro* account of the Medici branch in Venice was closed on August 17 and the balance was carried forward to another folio of the ledger. On that date there were only £86 7*s*. groat owing to the Venetian branch.

The entries in the ledger of the Bruges branch of the Medici bank throw light on a number of controversial points concerning the bill of exchange and the exchange contract. Since the exchange dealings of the Medici bank were probably typical and did not differ in character from those of other Italian merchant bankers, the facts disclosed by the Medici records should receive careful attention on the part of economic historians and legal writers. From this examination of the records, it clearly appears that:

a) Bills of exchange were always based on a real or fictitious exchange transaction

b) Bills of exchange, as a rule, were issued in one place and payable in another

c) Bills of exchange were not discounted but were bought and sold at a price which was determined by the rate of exchange. This price was nearly always indicated in the bill and in the bookkeeping records of the bankers

d) The merchant bankers did not charge interest, but that their profits (or losses) arose from disparities between the exchange rates. For example, the ducat was normally rated higher in Venice than in Bruges. The interest charges, of course, were hidden in the rates. However, since exchange rates were inherently unstable, profits were uncertain, but the lender had a slight advantage over the borrower. The business of exchange was essentially speculative and risky.

e) There existed in Bruges, Venice, and other commercial centers an organized money market; and exchange rates were market rates. Those who chose to use the mechanism of the money market had to follow the rules of the game

f) Bills were not negotiable but payable by the person named in the bill as the payor to the person designated as the payee. However, the lack of negotiability did not interfere in the least with the settlement of international debts by book transfer, thus eliminating specie completely

TABLE 5

VOSTRO OR LORO ACCOUNT OF THE VENETIAN BRANCH OF THE MEDICI BANK IN THE BOOKS OF THE BRUGES BRANCH

Debit Side

Explanation	Amount in Flemish Currency		
1441	£	*s.*	*d.*
Chosimo de'Medici e Conpagnia di Venegia per loro chonto qui deono dare a dì primo di giugno £ sessantacinque di grossi sono per la valuta di ducati 300 rimetemo loro detto dì per uso da Ghuglielmo da Chasasaggia chambiare chon Bartolomeo Riba a grossi 52 per ducato, posto detto dè avêre in questo a carta 206......................	65	0	0
E dì 5 di giugno £ settantanove s. sette d. undici di grossi sono per valuta di ducati 370 a grossi 51½ per ducato ci scrissono che per detto dì ne li facessimo debitore e creditore Piero Orco di Vinegia, posto detto dè avere in questo a carta 242................................	79	7	11
E dì 12 di giugno £ ottantotto s.tre d. quattro di grossi sono per valuta di scudi 419 di 66 [scudi al marco d'oro] rimettemo per loro a Ginevra a Giovanni Benci e Compagnia per la prossima fiera d'aghosto da Giorgio Chornero chambiare chon Marcho Chornero a grossi 50½ per scudo in somma di scudi 838 posto detto Marcho dè avere in somma di £176 s.6 d.7 in questo a carta 214.............	88	3	4
Several items omitted..	812	6	6
E dì 25 detto s. tre di grossi per chosto d'uno protesto e chopia di ducati 400 fatto a noi medesimi fino a dì nove detto per lettera di Niccolò di Bartolomeo a grossi 53 per ducato tornorono, posto Maruzio notaio, dè avere in questo a carta 196..........................		3	0
Four items omitted..	119	6	8
E dì 17 d'aghosto £86 s.7 di grossi posto deono avere in questo a carta 275 per resto di qui che ttanti restano avere a questo chonto....	86	7	0
	1,250	14	5

g) Unpaid bills were protested by notaries and were returned to the place of issue. There recourse was taken against the maker or drawer who had sold a worthless bill.

These remarks apply to the Italian bill of exchange or *lettera di pagamento* and not to the great variety of formal and informal credit instruments, such as bonds, bills of debt, recognizances, letters of assignment, and so forth, which were in use in the Northern trade. Such instruments often contained the payable-to-the-bearer clause, but their status was frequently uncertain at law. The Italian merchant bankers sometimes made advances on informal bills of debt and other instruments, as is evident from the records of the Borromei bank in London. In other words, the Italians adapted themselves to the usages and customs of the Northern trade.

A careful distinction, however, should be made between those Northern instruments and the Italian bill of exchange. The latter presupposes the existence of organized money markets, stereotyped forms, and well-established business practices, all of which were unknown to the Northern trade. The English merchants began to use the bill of exchange only toward the end of the fifteenth century, and their dealings were limited to London, Calais, and Bruges. One should not forget that the business practices of the Italians were far in advance of those of the other nations.

TABLE 5

Vostro or Loro Account of the Venetian Branch of the Medici Bank in the Books of the Bruges Branch

Credit Side

Explanation	Amount in Flemish Currency		
	£	s.	d.
1441			
Chosimo de' Medici e conpagnia di Vinegia per loro chonto qui deono avere a dì primo di giugno £ cinqueciento cinquanta quattro s. otto d. due di grossi posto deono dare in questo a carta 215 per resto di là che ttanti restavano avere a quello chonto........................	554	8	2
E dì 8 giugno £ cientotto s.sei d.otto di grossi sono per valuta di ducati 500 a grossi 52 per ducato ci scrissono per loro lettera di dì 20 d'aprile che per detto dì ne li facessimo creditore a questo chonto e debitore al conto per noi per la valuta chonti alloro medesimi per tanti ne manchava loro per noi, posto deono dare in questo a carta 195	108	6	8
E dì detto £79 s.7 d.11 di grossi sono per valuta di ducati 366 grossi 10½ scrivemo loro che da detto dì per uso ne facessino creditore Piero Horco da Vinegia per la valuta a grossi 52 per ducato chonti a noi medesimi per tanti ce n'avanzava per lui, posto dè dare in questo a carta 242..	79	7	11
E dì 27 di giugno £65 s.7 d.5 di grossi sono per valuta di ducati 301 grossi 17 a grossi [di Fiandra] 52 per ducato ci rimessono per detto dì da Bernardo Chambi e Conpagnia per lettera di Piero Ghuidacioni posto detto Bernardo dè dare in questo a carta 209......	65	7	5
E dì 6 di luglio £56 s.10 d.2 di grossi sono per valuta di ducati 250 a grossi 54¼ per ducato ci rimessono per detto dì da Giufredo Rapondi per lettera di Piero Souranzo, posto detto Giufredo dè dare in questo a carta 252..	56	10	2
Several items omitted..	386	14	1
	1,250	14	5

Source: Ledger of the Bruges branch, 1441, fol. 241.

VI. AN EXAMPLE OF DRY EXCHANGE

Dry exchange might be defined as a transaction involving exchange and re-exchange in which no real payment was made abroad. Such a transaction consequently involved two bills instead of one: one for the exchange and the other for the re-exchange. Usually an exchange transaction involved four parties: a deliverer and a taker in one place and a payor and a payee in another place. In the case of dry exchange the number of parties was reduced to three. The third party was usually at the same time payor and payee of the first bill and deliverer and taker of the second bill.

The account of Antonio di Niccolò del Conte of Venice gives us a good example of dry exchange. The Medici of Venice apparently bought from him a bill of 533 ducats. As he had neither correspondents nor balances abroad, he was told to draw a bill on the Medici of Bruges and to make it payable to the same. The Medici of Bruges thus were at the same time payor and payee. Probably the bill read: *pagate a voi medesimi* ("pay to yourselves").

When the bill arrived in Bruges and came to maturity, the Medici in this city "paid themselves" by simply debiting the account of del Conte and crediting the *Vostro* account of the Venetian branch with 533 ducats at 51½ groats per ducat or £114 10*s.* groat. The account of Antonio del Conte was then charged with 9 groats for consular fees at the rate of 2 mites or one-twelfth groat per £ and with 4*s.* 8*d.* for commission at the rate of two per thousand. Next, the Medici made out a new bill payable by del Conte to the Medici of Venice. This bill probably stated that the Medici had received the value "from themselves" (*per la valuta ricevuta da noi medesimi*), that is, by transfer in their own books. As a result, the entry made before was reversed: the account of Antonio del Conte was credited with £114 15*s.* 6*d.* groat, equivalent to 534⅞ ducats, and the account of the Venetian branch of the Medici was debited with the same amount.

The outcome was that the Medici of Venice had lent 533 ducats and recovered 534⅞ ducats at the end of four months or two usances. They made no profit on this transaction and received just enough more to cover the local charges in Bruges. The Medici of Venice just broke even because the ducat was rated at 51½ groats in both the first and the second bill. Had there been any disparity in the rates, there would have been either a profit or a loss. Normally, there was a profit, because the ducat was usually rated higher in Venice than in Bruges. The following statement shows how the profit was determined.

Case No. 1

	Pounds Groat £	s.	d.	Ducats of 24 *grossi*
Cost of first bill in Venice and proceeds in Bruges at 51½ gr. per ducat	114	10	0	533.0
Local charges in Bruges at 51½ per ducat		5	6	1.21
Total Cost	114	15	6	534.21
Proceeds of second bill at 51½ per ducat in Venice and cost in Bruges	114	15	6	534.21
Profit				0

The account of Antonio del Conte records two other transactions involving dry exchange. In both cases there is a profit because the ducat was not rated each time as high in Bruges as in Venice.

Case No. 2

	Pounds £	Groat s.	d.	Ducats of 24 *grossi*
Cost of first bill in Venice and proceeds in Bruges at 54½ gr. per ducat	85	14	5	377.17
Local charges in Bruges		7	7	1.17
Total	86	2	0	379.10
Cost of second bill in Bruges and proceeds in Venice at 51½ gr. per ducat	86	2	0	401.6
Profit				21.20

Case No. 3

	Pounds £	Groat s.	d.	Ducats of 24 *grossi*
Cost of first bill in Venice and proceeds in Bruges at 53¼ gr. per ducat	97	18	0	441.6
Local charges in Bruges		4	8	1.3
Total	98	2	8	442.9
Proceeds of second bill in Venice and cost in Bruges at 51 gr. per ducat	98	2	8	461.19
Profit				19.10

As these cases show, there was neither profit nor loss if the ducat was worth in Bruges as much as in Venice, but there was a profit if the ducat was rated higher in Venice than in Bruges and there was a loss if the ducat was rated higher in Bruges than in Venice. Moreover, the profit or loss increased or decreased with the discrepancy between the two rates, that is, the rate in Bruges and in Venice.

In the case of dry exchange, the bills were actually sent abroad. As these three cases show, profits still depended upon the whimsical behavior of the exchange rates and, as a result, were uncertain.

Fictitious exchange differed from dry exchange in that fictitious exchange was based either on fictitious bills or on fictitious rates. By fictitious bills, I mean that bills were made out *pro forma* but not actually sent abroad. By fictitious rates, one must understand rates other than market rates. The use of fictitious rates made it possible to eliminate all element of risk by determining in advance the rate of the second bill or, in other words, the rate at which returns would be made. Such fictitious exchange transactions were clearly illegal, and I have not found any example in the Medici records. As for dry exchange, this practice was doubtful in the fifteenth century and was not formally condemned until 1571 by Pope Pius V.

TABLE 6

Account of Antonio del Conte Concerning Dry Exchange

Debit Side

Explanation	Amount in Flemish Currency		
1441	£	s.	d.
Antonio di Niccholò del Chonte da Vinegia dè dare a dì 13 di maggio £ cientoquattordici s.dieci di grossi sono per la valuta di ducati 533 da Vinegia a grossi 51½ per ducato ci scrissono e' Medici di Vinegia per loro lettera di dì 30 di Marzo che per lo dì sopra di loro ne lo facessimo debitore e lloro creditore posto deone avere al chonto per loro sopra di loro in questo carta 215	114	10	0
E dì 12 di luglio d. nove di grossi sono per chonsolaggio de' Fiorentini a miti 2 per £ di questo chonto posto il chonsolato dè avere in questo a carta 264			9
E dì detto s. quattro d. otto di grossi sono per nostra provisione a 2 per mille di questo chonto posto provisione deono avere in questo a carta 220		4	8
E dì detto d.uno di grossi posto Boscio di Giovanni di Valenza per nostro chonto dè avere in questo a carta 132 per tanti ne manchava a quello chonto e avanzava a questo			1
E dì 15 di settenbre £ ottantacinque s. quattordici d. cinque di grossi sono per la valuta di ducati 377 grossi 17 a grossi 54½ per ducato scrissono e' Medici di Vinegia che per detto dì ne lo facessimo debitore e lloro creditore sopra li loro, posto deono avere in questo a carta 277	85	14	5
E dì 15 di gienaio £ novantasette s.18 di grossi sono per valuta di ducati 441¼ a grossi 53¼ per ducato scrissono e' Medici di Vinegia per loro lettera di dì 24 di novembre per detto dì ne lo facessimo sopra di loro debitore e lloro creditore, posto deono avere in questo a carta 316	97	18	0
E dì 24 di febraio s. uno d.tre di grossi sono per chonsolaggio de' Fiorentini a miti 2 per £, posto dè avere in questo a carta 309		1	3
E dì detto s.11 di grossi sono per nostra provisione a 2 per mille, posto provisione deono avere a carta 220		11	0
	299	0	2

TABLE 6

ACCOUNT OF ANTONIO DEL CONTE CONCERNING DRY EXCHANGE

Credit Side

Explanation	Amount in Flemish Currency		
1441	£	s.	d.
Antonio di Niccholò del Chonte da Vinegia dè avere a dì 15 di maggio £ cientoquattordici s. quindici d. sei di grossi sono per la valuta di ducati 534⅞ scrivemo a Vinegia a' Medici che da detto dì per uso ne lo facessono sopra di loro debitore e nnoi creditore qui al conto per loro per tanti cie ne manchava per detto, posto detti Medici per loro chonto deono dare in questo a carta 215........................	114	15	6
E dì 16 di settenbre £ ottantasei s. due di grossi sono per valuta di ducati 401¼ a grossi 51½ per ducato scrivemo a Vinegia a' Medici che da detto dì per uso ne lo facessino debitore e noi creditore qui al chonto per loro sopra di loro conti a noi medesimi per tanti ciene manchava per la valuta, posto deono dare in questo a carta 275......	86	2	0
E dì 18 di gienaio £98 s.2 d.8 di grossi sono per la valuta di ducati 461 grossi 19 scrivemo a Vinegia a' Medici che da dì 16 detto ne lo facessino debitore sopra di loro e creditore qui al conto per loro per tanti ciene manchava per detto, posto detti Medici deono dare in questo a carta 341..	98	2	8
	299	0	2

Source: Ledger of Bruges branch, fol. 231.

VII. THE ACCOUNT OF THE BRUGES MONEY-CHANGER, SIMON DE COKERE

This money-changer is called Simone de Coccho, *cambiatore,* in the ledger of the Medici branch in Bruges. The Medici apparently dealt with Simon de Cokere only occasionally, and there was no continuous business connection. However, they sometimes made payments by transfer in the books of Simon de Cokere. For example, on May 27, 1441, they asked him to credit £30 to Paolo Spinola and promised to supply him the necessary funds. As a matter of fact, Simon de Cokere transferred £22 to the credit of the Medici on the same day and collected the balance of £8 in cash three days later, on May 30.

On August 7, an innkeeper, John Leclerq, upon orders from Nicholas de Drijl of Brussels, ordered Simon de Cokere to transfer £50 to the credit of the Medici. The Medici withdrew this money in cash within two days. Apparently they did not care to keep an account with Simon de Cokere. The same happened on December 23, when a Catalan, Bartolomeo Riba, paid the Medici by transfer in bank. They were prompt to withdraw their credit in cash.

Simon de Cokere failed in 1453. Because of numerous bank failures, the monetary ordinances of the fifteenth century forbade the money-changers to accept on deposit the money of the merchants and to make their payments, presumably by book transfer. The entries in the Medici ledgers show that those

TABLE 7

ACCOUNT OF THE BRUGES MONEY-CHANGER, SIMON DE COKERE

Debit Side

Explanation	Amount in Flemish Currency		
1441	£	s.	d.
Simone de Choccho [de Cokere], chambiatore, dè dare a dì 27 di maggio £ ventidue di grossi ebbe per noi da Cholardo Dalto, posto dè avere in questo a carta 223..................................	22	0	0
E dì 30 di maggio £ otto di grossi paghamoli contanti, portò il suo chericho, per resto di suo chonto a uscita carta 80, posto la chassa dè avere in questo a carta 236..................................	8	0	0
E dì 7 d'aghosto £ cinquanta di grossi promisseci per Giovani Leclerch oste "a la Chopa" el quale cie li fe dare per Niccolò Dederil [de Drijl] da Borsella, posto detto Niccolò dè avere in questo a carta 221	50	0	0
E dì 23 di dicembre £ ciento di grossi promisseci per Bartolomeo Riba, Chatalano, a entrata carta 40, posto dè avere in questo a carta 310	100	0	0
	180	0	0

Credit Side

Explanation	Amount in Flemish Currency		
1441	£	s.	d.
Simone de Choccho, chambiatore, dè avere a dì 27 di maggio £ trenta di grossi promettemoli per Paolo Spinola da Gienova, posto dè dare in questo a carta 209..	30	0	0
E dì 9 d'aghosto £ cinquanta di grossi avemo dallui chontanti rechò Attaviano nostro a entrata carta 35, posto la chassa dè dare in questo a carta 255..	50	0	0
E dì 25 di dicenbre £ ciento di grossi avemo da lui chontanti in due partite, cioè £85 e 15 rechò Attaviano nostro a entrata carta 40, posto la chassa dè dare in questo carta 311.......................	100	0	0
	180	0	0

Source: Ledger of Bruges branch, fol. 238.

enactments were disregarded and that the money-changers, despite the ordinances, continued to accept deposits and to transfer funds. However, the money-changing business was on the decline in the fifteenth century. Later enactments added teeth to the law and heavy fines were imposed both on money-changers and merchants who dared to violate the regulations. These measures eventually killed the banking business of the Bruges money-changers: it disappeared completely by 1500.

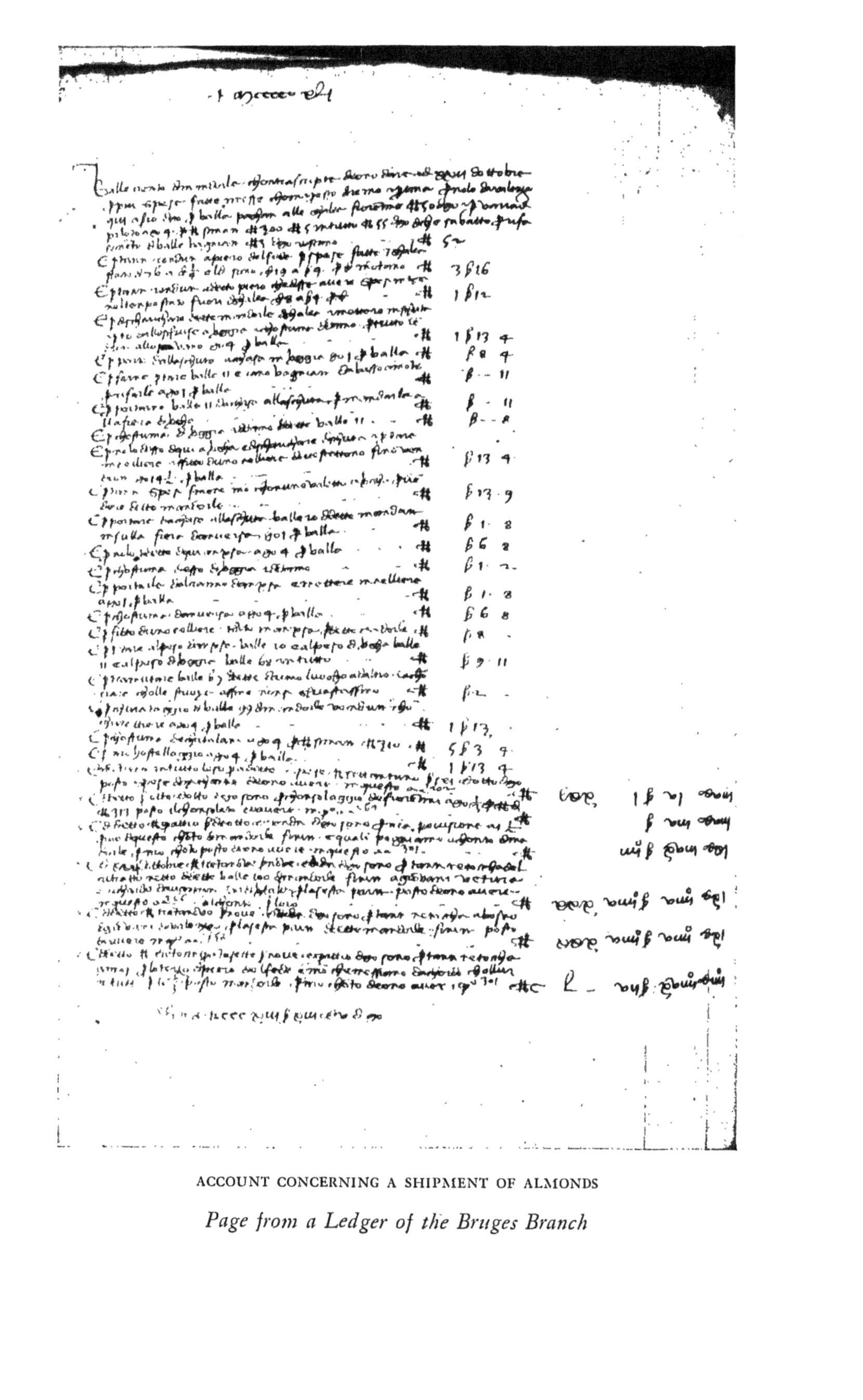

ACCOUNT CONCERNING A SHIPMENT OF ALMONDS

Page from a Ledger of the Bruges Branch

VIII. ACCOUNT OF THE ONE HUNDRED BALES OF ALMONDS

The chief interest of this account resides in the fact that it gives an itemized and detailed statement of all the charges incurred by the Medici branch in Bruges in connection with a shipment of 100 bales of almonds from Valencia to Bruges. This transaction has been discussed in the text and it will suffice to give here a translation of the Italian entries in the Medici ledger, since there are no problems of interpretation and since the entries are important and significant only because of the detailed information which they give on charges, rates, tariffs, and business customs.

"One hundred bales of almonds owe on October 22 [1441] for several expenses incurred in connection with the same as will be stated hereafter: and first, for freight from Valencia to here at 10*s.* groat per bale, paid to the Florentine galleys, £50 groat; and for pilotage at 4 groats per pound, on the basis of an estimated value of £300, £5; in all, £55 groat from which are to be deducted £3 groat for damages to water-soaked bales, leaving .... £52 gr.

"And for so much owing to Piero del Fede for expenses on board of the galley, viz.: *dobbre* 76 at ¼ ducat for each *dobbra* make 19 ducats, at 4s. groat per ducat, amount to .... £3 16*s.* gr.

"And for so much owing to Piero as he said that he had spent for charges on land, while the bales were outside the galleys, 8 ducats at 4*s.* gr. per ducat, amount to .... £1 12*s.* gr.

"And for unloading the said almonds from the galleys, and for transhipment into the barges or *schuiten,* and for freight from Sluys to Bruges, and for the customs of Damme, all repaid to the scribe [of the galleys] 4 groats per bale .... £1 13*s.* 4*d.* gr.

"And for cartage from the *schuit* or barge to the warehouse in Bruges, 1 groat per bale .... 8*s.* 4*d.*

"And for carrying 11 water-soaked bales upstairs [to an attic?], to dry, at 1 groat per bale .... 11*d.*

"And for cartage of 11 bales from the warehouse to the *schuit* to be shipped to the fair of Bergen-op-Zoom .... 11*d.*

"And for the customs of Bruges and Damme on the said 11 bales .... 8*d.*

"And for freight from here to Bergen-op-Zoom, and for unloading from the barge, and for carrying to a cellar, and for rent of the cellar where [the bales] were stored until sold, 14½ groats per bale .... 13s.4*d.*

"And for expenses because we went with a clerk to Bergen-op-Zoom to sell the said almonds .... 13*s.* 9*d.*

"And for cartage from the warehouse to the barge of 20 bales of the said almonds shipped to the fair of Antwerp, 1 groat per bale .... 1*s.* 8*d.*

"And for freight from here to Antwerp, 4 groats per bale .... 6*s.*8*d.*

"And for customs of Bruges and Damme on the same .... 1*s.* 2*d.*

"And for cartage from the river at Antwerp and for storing in a cellar, at one groat per bale .... 1*s.* 8*d.*

"And for the customs of Antwerp at 4 groats per bale .... 6*s.*8*d.*

"And for rent of a cellar in Antwerp to store the said almonds .... 8*s.*

TABLE 8

Debit Side of an Account Concerning a Shipment of One Hundred Bales of Almonds

Explanation	Amount in Flemish Currency		
	£	s.	d.
1441			
Balle ciento di mandorle chontrascripte deono dare a dì 22 d'ottobre per più spese fatte in esse chom apresso diremo, e prima per nolo da Valenza qui a s. 10 di grossi per balla paghati alle ghalee fiorentine £50 di grossi, e per varra di piloto a grossi 4 per £, stimate 300 £, £5, in tutto £55 di grossi di che s'abatte per rifacimento di balle bagniate £3 di grossi, restano..................................	52	0	0
E per tanti renduti a Piero del Fede per spese fatte in ghalea, stato dobbre 76 a ducato ¼ el dobbra sono ducati 19 a soldi 4 [moneta di Fiandra] per ducato, montano..................................	3	16	0
E per tanti renduti a detto Piero che disse avere spese in terra nel tenpo fuori di ghalea ducati 8, a s.4 per ducato, montano............	1	12	0
E per dischariare dette mandorle di ghalea e mettere in schuta [barca, dal fiammingo schuit], e porto dalle Schiuse a Bruggia, e chostuma di Damo, per tutto renduti allo scrivano, grossi 4 per balla..	1	13	4
E per porto dalla schuta a chassa in Bruggia, grosso 1 per balla....		8	4
E per farne portare balle 11, erano bagniate, da basso a monte, per rifarle a grosso 1 per balla..................................			11
E per portarne balle 11 da chasa alla schuta per mandarle alla fiera di Bergha [Bergen-op-Zoom]..................................			11
E per chostuma di Bruggia e di Damo di dette balle 11..........			8
E per nolo d'esse di qui a Bergha, e dischariare di schuta, e per dare in celliere, e fitto d'uno celliere dove stettono fino vendute grossi 14½ per balla..................................		13	4
E per tante spese smovemmo chon uno valetto a Bergha per vendere dette mandorle..................................		13	9
E per portare da chasa alla schuta balle 20 di dette mandate in sulla fiera d'Anversa grosso 1 per balla....................		1	8
E per nolo di dette di qui [a] Anversa a grossi 4 per balla........		6	8
E per chostuma d'esse di Bruggia e di Damo..................		1	2
E per portarle dal ramo d'Anversa e mettere in celliere a grosso 1 per balla..................................		1	8
E per chostuma d'Anversa a grossi 4 per balla.................		6	8
E per fitto d'uno celliere tolto in Anversa per dette mandorle......		8	0
E per portare al peso d'Anversa balle 20, e al peso di Bergha balle 11, e al peso di Bruggia balle 68, in tutto......................		9	11
E per tramutare balle 69 di dette da uno luogho ad altro e achonciare colle stuoye affine non si ghuastassino..................		2	0
E per churatággio di balle 99 di mandorle vendute chon churattiere a grossi 4 per balla..................................	1	13	0
E per chostuma de'Chatalani a grossi 4 per £, stimati £310.....	5	3	4
E per nostro hostellaggio a grossi 4 per balla.................	1	13	4
E montano in tutto le sopradette spese £ 71 s.6 d.8 di grossi, posto spese di merchantie deono avere in questo a carta 202........	71	6	8
E dì detto s.8 d.8 di grossi, sono per chonsolaggio de'Fiorentini a grossi ⅓ per £, di £ 313, posto il chonsolato dè avere in questo a carta 264..................................		8	8
E dì detto £4 s.18 d.11 di grossi sono per nostra provisione a 1½ per 100 di questo conto di mandorle finiti, e quali pogniamo a chonto di mandorle per nostro chonto, posto deono avere in questo a carta 301	4	18	11
Total	76	14	3

TABLE 8

ACCOUNT CONCERNING A SHIPMENT OF ONE HUNDRED BALES OF ALMONDS

(Continued)

Explanation	Amount in Flemish Currency		
	£	s.	d.
[Carried forward]	76	14	3
E dì 22 d'ottobre £39 s.9 d.11 di grossi sono per tanti ne toccha del ritratto netto di dette balle 100 di mandorle finite a Giovanni Ventura e Richardo Davanzati e Conpagnia di Barzalona per la sesta parte, poste deono avere in questo a carta 266 al chonto per loro......	39	9	11
E dì detto £39 s.9 d.11 di grossi sono per tanti ne toccha a Bosco di Giovanni di Valenza per la sesta parte di dette mandorle finite, posto dè avere in questo a carta 158........................	39	9	11
E dì detto £157 s.19 d.4 di grossi sono per tanti ne toccha a nnoi per lo terzo di Piero del Fede e nostro mettiamo d'achordo chollui in tutto per li ⅔, posto mandorle per nostro chonto deono avere in questo carta 301..	157	19	4
Somma	313	13	5

Source: Ledger of the Bruges branch, fol. 246.

"And for carrying 20 bales to the weighhouse in Antwerp, 11 bales to the weighhouse in Bergen-op-Zoom, and 68 bales to the weighhouse in Bruges, in all .... 9*s.* 11*d.*

"And for spreading out on mats the contents of 69 bales and stirring them so that they would not spoil .... 2*s.*

"And for brokerage of 99 bales of almonds sold through brokers at 4 groats per bale .... £1 13*s.*

"And for the Catalan customs at 4 groats per pound on an estimate of £310 gr. .... £5 3*s.* 4*d.*

"And for our storage charges at 4 groats per bale .... £1 13*s.*4*d.*

"And the foresaid expenses amount in all to £71 6*s.* 8*d.* groat, posted to Merchandise Expense must have, in this ledger on folio 202 .... £71 6*s.*8*d.*

"And on the said day 8*s.* 8*d.* gr. for the Florentine consular fees at ⅓ groat per £, on £313 gr., posted the said Consulate must have, in this ledger on fol. 264 .... 8*s.* 8*d.*

"And on the said day £4 18*s.* 11*d.* groat for our commission at 1½ per cent on the almonds sold which we post to the credit of the almonds sold for our own account, in this ledger on fol. 301 .... £4 18*s.* 11*d.*

Total .... £76 14*s.* 3*d.*"

There are three more entries on the debit side of the almonds account. They deal with the allocation of the proceeds among the partners to this joint venture in which the Medici had originally only a one-third interest.

The entries on the credit side of the account all deal with the sale of the almonds. These entries all resemble each other and are of no great interest, except the first of which an English translation is given here:

"One hundred bales of almonds belonging for one-third to Piero del Fede, for another third to us, and for the rest to Giovanni Ventura and Ricardo Davanzati and Company of Barcelona and to Bosco di Giovanni of Valencia must have on June 19, 1441, £50 16*s.* 6*d.* groat which we received in cash from Thomas Englishman by our Simone. These are the proceeds of 17 bales of almonds sold to him [Thomas] at 16*s.* groat the hundred [lbs.], and they weigh as appear in the Memorandum book on folio 9, 6,574 lbs., tare at 17 lbs. per bale or 289 lbs., remain net 6,285 lbs., and for wrappers, at 8 gr. each, 11*s.* 4*d.* gr., at Receipts, fol. 33, posted to the debit of Cash in this ledger fol. 244 .... £50 16*s.* 6*d.*"

IX. THE PORTRAIT OF FRANCESCO SASSETTI WITH HIS SON TEODORO IN THE BACHE COLLECTION OF THE METROPOLITAN MUSEUM OF ART

For several decades there has been confusion in the identification of the son shown with Francesco in the Ghirlandajo portrait, which is now in the Bache collection of the Metropolitan Museum. An inscription in Latin across the top of the painting states that it shows Francesco Sassetti and his son, Teodoro. But Francesco had two sons named Teodoro: his eldest son, who was born in 1460 and who died in 1479, and his youngest son, born the year of his brother's death and, following a custom of the time, named for the deceased child.

In an article on Francesco Sassetti, first published in 1907, Aby Warburg stated that the Teodoro shown in the painting was Francesco's youngest son.[1] Most reproductions of the painting have a label based on Warburg's identification of the boy as Teodoro II.

But the appearance of the two figures and the dates of Francesco and his sons make this identification obviously wrong. The youth in the painting might be seven to ten years of age and the man appears to be in his early forties. Francesco, born in 1420, was forty years old when his eldest son Teodoro was born and fifty-nine when Teodoro II was born. Were the son in the portrait the younger Teodoro, his father would have to be a man in his late sixties. Ghirlandajo did portray Sassetti in his sixties in the fresco which decorates the walls of the Sassetti Chapel in Santa Trinità in Florence. In that fresco, a young boy, apparently the second Teodoro, stands beside his father who is clearly an elderly man.

If the boy in the painting in the Metropolitan Museum is the first Teodoro, then Francesco would have been in his late forties at the time he was portrayed with his eldest son. Yet the adult figure in the painting looks somewhat younger than the marble bust of Francesco Sassetti, from the workshop of Antonio Rossellini, on which it is stated that Sassetti is forty-four years of age. That would give the date of 1464 to the bust that makes Sassetti look like an ancient Roman (see illustration opposite page 8). Allowing for the difference in

[1] Warburg, "Francesco Sassettis letztwillige Verfügung," *Gesammelte Schriften,* I, 132 n. 5. The dates of Sassetti's five sons are given on p. 131: Teodoro (1460–1479), Galeazzo (1462–1513), Cosimo (1463–1527), Federigo (1472–1490), and Teodoro II (1479–1546).

medium and in manner, it is still possible to accept a date in the late 1460's for the painting.[2]

This would make the portrait a youthful work of Ghirlandajo, but art historians have attributed the painting, on the basis of style, to the 1480's. Some have questioned whether it is by the hand of Ghirlandajo himself.

In recent correspondence, Professor Richard Offner of New York University, an authority on Florentine painting, suggested an explanation that seems to solve the problem of relating the painting to both the 1460's and the 1480's. Domenico Ghirlandajo, in his youth, apparently painted Francesco Sassetti and his eldest son, Teodoro. But in the 1480's a replica of the painting was made in Ghirlandajo's workshop. The hand of the master did some of the work, but an assistant did most of it. It is the replica that is in the Bache Collection. The original apparently is lost. Perhaps it had been damaged and so a replica was commissioned after the elder Teodoro's death in order to preserve a likeness of the deceased son.

In any case, it appears that the Bache painting should be labeled "Francesco Sassetti and his son, Teodoro I." Possibly it should be designated as a copy, from the workshop of Domenico Ghirlandajo, of an early original by the master.

[2] The face of Francesco Sassetti in the Ghirlandajo portrait has a very wooden expression. The restorer of the Metropolitan Museum is convinced that the face has been retouched. The Museum plans eventually to restore the picture to its original state.

INDEX

www.ingramcontent.com/pod-product-compliance
Lightning Source LLC
LaVergne TN
LVHW020636100826
845148LV00012B/2206

* 9 7 8 1 5 9 7 4 0 3 8 1 8 *